Books by Sanaya Roman

A   *Living with Joy: Keys to Personal Power and Spiritual Transformation*
Book I of the Earth Life Series

A+ *Personal Power through Awareness: A Guidebook for Sensitive People*
Book II of the Earth Life Series

A   *Spiritual Growth: Being Your Higher Self*
Book III of the Earth Life Series

B   Soul Love : AWAKENING YOUR HEART CHAKRAS

Books by Sanaya Roman and Duane Packer, Ph.D.

A– *Opening to Channel: How to Connect with Your Guide*

A   *Creating Money: Keys to Abundance*

To all of you discovering
the oneness of the whole
and the wholeness of the one.

Sanaya Roman
CHANNEL FOR ORIN

Personal Power
through
Awareness

A GUIDEBOOK FOR
SENSITIVE PEOPLE

H J Kramer Inc
Tiburon, California

H J Kramer Inc, Publishers
P.O. Box 1082
Tiburon, California 94920

Library of Congress Cataloging-in-Publication Data

Orin (Spirit)
    Personal power through awareness : a guidebook for sensitive people /
Sanaya Roman, channel for Orin.
        p. cm. — (Earth life series ; bk. 2)
    "Taught by Orin, a wise and gentle spirit teacher channeled by Sanaya
Roman" — Cover p. [4].
    ISBN 0-915811-04-9 : $12.95
    1. Spirit writings.   2. Self-realization — Miscellanea.
3. Telepathy.   I. Roman, Sanaya.   II. Title.   III. Series: Orin (Spirit).
Earth life series : bk. 2.
BF 1301.072 1990
133.9'3 — dc20   89-15249
                                                                       CIP

Cover painting "E = MC^2" © 1986 by Judith Cornell, Ph.D.
Light is a theme that appears in the great
spiritual teachings of all ages.

Book design by Abigail Johnston
Composition by Curt Chelin

First paperback edition 1986
Manufactured in the United States of America
20   19   18   17   16

ACKNOWLEDGMENTS

I wish to express my gratitude to Duane Packer, PhD for his help and support in these books, and for our work of joy together channeling and teaching.

My heartfelt appreciation goes to LaUna Huffines for her support of Orin and myself, and for her book, *Connecting*, which has helped me express more love. I want to especially thank Ed and Amerinda Alpern for their many contributions to my life and Orin's work. I also wish to thank Linda Johnston, Wendy Grace, Scotta Catamas, Cheryl Williams, Jeff Abbott, Nancy and Sara McJunkin, Sandy Hobson, Lisa Benson, Rob and Stacey Friedman, Evelyn Taylor, Debra Ross, Shirley Runco, Karen La Puma, and Linda Lutzkendorf. I want to thank you who have been holding a vision during this time for Orin's books and our learning together: Jan Shelley, Eva Roza, Mary Beth Braun, Leah Warren, Mari Ane Anderson, Mary Pat Mahan, Rosemary Crane, Sylvia Larson, Colleen Hicks, Trudie London, Carol Hawkinson, Roberta Heath, Jill O'Hara, Patrice Noli, and Dona Crowder. I want to acknowledge all of you who have supported Orin for your presence, love, and support; and the channeling community for your wisdom and willingness to grow.

I want to thank my editor, Elaine Ratner, for her excellent editing, Abigail Johnston for her assistance in design, and

Lois Landau for her conscientious typing. I want to thank Hal Kramer for his support and for making these books a reality. I also want to thank Rob for his encouragement and love; my parents, Court and Shirley Smith, for their guidance; Otto and Ruth Brown, and Dorothy Lundy for their constant love, and my brothers and sisters, David, Debra, Patricia, and Robert.

I want to acknowledge Seth, Jane Roberts, and Robert Butts for the contribution their books have made to my life; Dick Sutphen for his books and tapes; and others who are helping people awaken to their full potential such as Shirley Maclaine, Carlos Castenadas, Richard Bach, Edgar Cayce, and Betty Bethards.

My deepest love and appreciation goes to the Masters and Beings of Light whose presence has enabled all of us to reach more light.

CONTENTS

I

Greetings
From Orin

I invite you to explore with me the universe you know so well. We will view it from a slightly different perspective, in a way that allows it to take on an added dimension, an unsuspected richness. It is the world of energy that exists all around you. This book will enable you to see more clearly the energy world you exist in, to understand the belief systems, mass thoughtforms, and telepathic energies of others which affect you. It is a course in bringing the unconscious into consciousness, delving into the mystery of the unseen energies in and around you. There is much beyond what you see with your five senses, and it can affect you. As you understand these unseen energies, they can become a tool to assist you in getting to wherever you want to go.

Looking at energy closely is like looking at a familiar object through a microscope. Although it is still the same object, it looks different up close. This course will act like a microscope, helping you view the unseen energies around you in greater detail, turning and adjusting the focus to provide a different perspective. It is the same world you have always known, but as you understand and perceive it in new ways it will reveal its secrets to you.

You *can learn to recognize the energies you pick up subconsciously.*

The microscope, in this case, is your awareness, your innate ability to focus your attention on whatever you choose. Not only do you perceive the world through your physical senses, you also pick up information constantly at a nonverbal, intuitive level. Your thoughts are the doorway to sensing energy, and your inner eyes provide the tools for changing and working with it. You can learn to heal negative energy, to increase your ability to visualize, and to have telepathic communication with people, knowing what they are thinking of you and how to work with their nonverbal messages. We will be working with your inner world. Part of sensing energy is hearing the messages all around you. You need not be affected by other people's bad moods. You have the ability to heal every time you notice negativity, to help people evolve, to increase the positive energy around you, and change the nature of your personal relationships.

You *are like a radio that can receive many stations. What you receive depends on what you pay attention to.*

Many energies exist that affect you throughout the day. You are also a broadcasting station, with a home base, a frequency, and a mind set. The way you perceive, judge, and react to your thoughts throughout the day grounds you in your reality and is the basis upon which that reality is created. As you become thoroughly familiar with your reality, you may leave it, for there are many realities you may step into once you are familiar with your own home station. You have a greater identity than you can imagine; you can unlock your present identity to experience even more of the richness of who you are.

Because you are like a radio, you can learn to set the dial and receive whatever information you want. You are telepathic; you receive and send messages all the time. In this book you will learn how to control the messages you pick up, choosing what you want to hear, and letting go of broadcasts you do not want to receive. You will learn how to tune into other people's energies, to assist and heal them, and to come from a place of greater understanding. If you want to become successful, if you want to experience greater peace and love between you and other people, if you want to move out of the denser energies into the finer ones, you can learn to do so. You can learn to identify thoughts and feelings from others you do not want to tune into, turning off their broadcast and linking with the higher energies of the universe instead. You will learn to open your intuition, that ability to sense and understand events at a deeper level, and open to receive guidance and answers to your questions.

The information and concepts in this book are presented in a way that will help you open to a deeper part of your being, triggering the memory of this and much more knowledge that already resides within you. You may experience my energy behind the words, which will help bring out the buried knowledge in you, awakening parts of you which have been slumbering. You meet these parts of yourself frequently in your dream state. You can bring them into your normal, waking consciousness.

Mankind as a species is awakening to many new abilities. These abilities are part of the evolutionary journey of man. The human aura—the energy surrounding the body—is evolving. With this evolution comes the ability to sense what used to be unseen, invisible energy. That energy can now be recognized, interpreted and directed; that which was unseen and unrecognized can now be visible and known.

You are evolving rapidly, and the evolutionary journey of man is continuing to take a leap forward. When you look back into the days of the Neanderthal and Cro-Magnon man you can see your bodies have changed; your ability to sense energy has changed radically also. Even the five senses have changed. For instance, earlier man did not have the ability to see all the colors you can see today.

Your energy centers are opening, your ability to be aware of and affected by previously invisible and unseen energies is increasing.

You can learn how to use these newly awakened senses. They are already awakening and present in you or you would not be called to this information. I am acting as a guide, one who has traveled before in these realms of energy that you are beginning to explore. Things such as telepathy, precognition, the ability to tap into new scientific inventions, discoveries of information not yet known, and an increased connection with universal consciousness will become the norm as evolution takes its course. The awakening of man is a journey into awareness of the higher energy realms. It is possible now for many to learn what was before only possible for a few. The awareness that used to take years of training in special techniques and meditation to develop is now possible for many to achieve without years of special preparation. The evolutionary journey is one of awakening consciousness, and I will help you in this course to discover, understand, and nurture the awakening that is already present within you. If you are drawn to this information, then you are certainly developing and experiencing your latent abilities. You can use them to operate more efficiently in your everyday world, coming from your higher self and creating immediate changes in your life.

Many of you grew up as very aware, sensitive children.

Many of you grew up in environments that often seemed inexplicable, in situations that did not seem to match who you are. Some of you felt different from those around you, as if you had an added dimension of awareness that other people did not have. Many of you felt emotionally sensitive, and it may have seemed that things that did not bother other people affected you greatly. You often did not know what was you and what was other people. Because you were telepathic and emotionally sensitive, you may have taken in other people's feelings and emotions and thought they were your own.

Most of you are gentle, loving, and sensitive, wanting to develop your personal power in ways that honor both yourself and others. Many of you had painful childhoods, not understanding how to deal with the rigidity or negativity you found around you. Often you were not recognized for who you are—a being of light and love wanting an opportunity to spread that joyful abundance of spirit. You who are evolving this new "sixth sense" are on a rapid path of growth, and need to discover your own uniqueness and skills.

As you open, it is important
to develop wisdom, release pain,
and rise above negativity.

As you begin sensing and interpreting the subtler and unseen energies of the universe, you will be developing the skill to know which energies to let become a part of you and which to release. I will show you how to be unaffected by the pain and negativity in other people, how to help yourself and others rise above it, and how to reach and connect with your higher self. As you grow more aware of what you are sensing, you also have the opportunity to become more aware of your higher self, and the guidance that is available to you from the higher realms of the universe.

You can open to your greater consciousness, travel into dimensions and realms that have not yet been explored, see yourself in larger and expanded ways. You can learn to see and understand who you really are, and begin to find answers to questions such as "Why am I here?" and "What is the meaning of life?" As you explore and awaken to these subtle energies, many doors will open and many new worlds will be there for you to discover.

I invite you to explore your greater being, to use your sensitivity to know the magnificence of who you are. Join with me. Explore your inner guidance and higher self as we journey together into the higher realms of the universe.

In love and light,
Orin

II

Sensing Energy

As you read this, sit in a comfortable position. Use every sense you have. Feel your breathing in your chest, face, mouth, and throat. You have many faculties for sensing energy; it is only a matter of paying attention to them. For a moment, listen to every sound in the room and outside of it. Become aware of your sense of smell, of touch, of the feeling of the clothing on your body, of what you are sitting on. Pay attention to any taste in your mouth. Close your eyes and think of all the things you have looked at today, as if everything you saw was in a movie you went to. What pictures did you put on your movie screen today?

Besides these familiar senses, you have another faculty you use all the time—your ability to sense energy. You use it whether you are consciously aware of it or not. You make decisions based upon the energy you sense. As you closed your eyes to think of the things you saw today, you used a process called visualization. You ran a movie inside your mind, reliving and reseeing what happened. In the same way, you can close your eyes and think of a rose, imagining that you are smelling its delicate fragrance, envisioning the color and the shape of it. You can picture sticking out your tongue and tasting it. All of this happens inside your mind. The ability to sense energy comes from the same place.

Each of you has the ability to visualize, for I believe everyone can think of a rose, either to picture it or feel it. This is the process you will use to become aware of the energy you live around. You can learn to feel the emotional energy in a room of people, picking out which person is emitting energy that feels like anxiety, upset, or joy. You can learn to change the effect of that energy by closing your eyes, focusing with precision on the energy that is bothering you, and changing its impact with your mind. Just as you can close your eyes and visualize a rose, so can you use the process of visualization to heal people and work on energy that you do not like, or would like to evolve.

The process of visualization can transform energy from negative to positive.

It is a process of becoming aware of your inner being. You have what I call inner eyes. You will use your inner eyes to sense energy. Your inner vision can work in many different ways. Some of you are able to picture the rose, some of you simply have a sense of it. Each of you has your own method of visualizing energy; there is no one right way to sense it.

To be able to sense energy, you need to be aware of your

self, and be able to clear your mental and emotional slate. If you saw a movie on a screen that had many crayon marks on it, the image on the screen would be jumbled rather than clear. To read energy, first clear your inner screen. For a moment, close your eyes and imagine that you have a clear white screen in your mind. A simple exercise to do before you sense energy is to take a deep breath and imagine energy coming from the bottom of your feet up through the top of your head and out into the universe. Then imagine a clear light from the universe coming straight down from above, into your head, and out through your feet. Picture warmth spreading throughout your body. Let yourself feel light and free all over. This is an exercise for relaxation, for it is only when you are relaxed that you are able to sense energy clearly. Tension in any form obscures clarity and blocks telepathic reception. Negative emotions will block an accurate picture. In fact, if you are feeling any negative energy when you begin to sense energy, this will draw the negative energy to you from others. Clear yourself out by creating a state of relaxation and peace. Your image of the white screen will create the state of mind that you need, and deep breathing will clear your emotions. Practice creating a state of relaxation. You can do it in a second. If you walk into any place—a bus, a restaurant, a grocery store—where you sense the energy is not to your liking, don't allow that energy to activate the part of you that does not like it. That would increase its effect on you.

Most of you tense up when you encounter negative energy. That attracts even more negative energy. To avoid being affected by negative energy, relax. Any process of relaxation will work. Then visualize or imagine a peaceful feeling. By visualizing what feelings you want, you will not pick up negative energy.

Suppose you walk into a room and you are thinking of a person you are angry at, or you are lost in thoughts of something else. You are not in present time or aware of your surroundings. The emotions that go along with your thoughts will magnetize similar emotions from people around you. If you walk into a restaurant and you are feeling bad about something you did, fairly soon you will feel even worse. For just as if you were a receiving station, you will connect with everyone in the room who is feeling the same emotional energy. You will surely and clearly pull it into yourself.

On the other hand, you can, if you want, use group energy on buses, in restaurants, or anywhere, to go to higher levels of thought or emotion. Try walking in with wonderful thoughts. You will begin to connect with the wonderful feelings of those around you, which will magnify your own ability to feel good. You will also amplify others' good feelings.

In every home are the energies and thoughts of the occupants.

What effect do people have when they walk into your home? Most visitors in your home add to the positive energy in it, for most people focus on those things that they like and admire. But if critical people come in and think, "How ugly this is, how bad this is," they contribute to the negative energy in your home. Be aware of what kind of people you invite into your home.

Everything you live around is charged with your thoughts and energy. Every time you look at your house and think, "This is too small; I don't like it," you send that energy into your house. It will be there to help bring you down. Every time you say, "What a wonderful place I live in, how fortunate I am to have this place," you make your home your friend and ally. Then, at times when you are not feeling good, you will find solace and comfort in your home. Hating something ties you to it, and if you want to move to a better place, start by loving what you have.

Watch how you respond when you handle those mundane things that come up every day. Every time you tense up when a light bulb goes out, or get upset when your car makes a strange noise, you create a tension that becomes a magnetic force and draws to you the next wrong thing. Tension or upset in your body magnetizes more problems to you. If when you first hear a strange noise in your car, you relax, put a smile in your heart and on your face, you avoid creating more negative energy in the future. I am not saying you won't have to handle the problem that is there, but you will have stopped yourself from creating a new problem. Learn to focus in on present-time and be aware of your environment.

You are constantly being sent signs from the universe about what path to take.

Not only are you surrounded by energy that can affect you negatively or positively, you are always being sent guidance. You can learn to read and interpret the messages to help you make the decisions you need to make. Part of sensing energy is learning to hear the messages all around you. There are telepathic messages in your relationships with your loved ones, wives or husbands, with your coworkers, bosses, or employees. There are many ways in which you can be aware of their energy.

Your thoughts are the doorway to sensing energy, and your inner eyes provide the tools for changing and working with it. I will teach you how to heal negative energy, to evolve your ability to visualize, and have telepathic communication with people, knowing what they are saying to you and how to work with their messages. We will be working with the world of inner images.

Each of you has a different way of sensing energy. Some of you see auras as color; others see them as feelings or thoughts about people. Some of you are not aware of what you are doing when you sense energy but realize it later. To sense energy accurately, learn to quiet your own self, step outside your thoughts, feelings, and emotions, and become a blank screen so that you can read impressions. Learn to know who you are. Just as you can pay attention to the sounds in a room and nothing else, so can you pay attention to the telepathic and unseen energy that is also there.

First, you will want to find out how your inner eyes work. When you hold an object do you sense a feeling, color, word, image? Each of you uses a different method; learn to recognize your own processes. Some of you sense energy by becoming highly emotional, some of you by creating mental images and pictures. Discover this week how you sense energy, and learn to create from it. You may be reacting to the energy you sense without conscious awareness of it. I hope to assist you in becoming consciously aware of it.

All of you have the ability to heal every time you notice negative energy, to help people evolve, to increase the positive energy in your homes and change the nature of your personal relationships. You need not be affected by other people's bad moods, be they mechanics or clerks, coworkers or supervisors, waitresses or advisors. If you are a clerk, waiter, mechanic, or supervisor, you can learn how not to be affected by the moods or behavior of the people you connect with all day. People can bring you down and make your life harder—or give you an opportunity to heal them. This week, whenever you go into a place and you notice you do not like the way you feel there, STOP. Become a blank screen, and relax. Think of how you want to feel, and begin to visualize yourself as feeling that way.

PLAYSHEET

1 | Sit quietly, clear your mind, and imagine a blank screen. Think of a rose. How do you picture it? Can you imagine touching, smelling, or tasting it?

2 | Think of the home you live in. What kinds of thoughts do you have about it? Send it thoughts of how much you love it.

3 | Practice relaxing. Take a deep breath and picture warmth and lightness spreading throughout your body. Mentally go through your body and observe any areas of tension. Let those areas relax. Practice relaxing yourself at least two more times today. See if you can become more aware of your body when it tenses up, and then consciously create relaxation.

III

Understanding and Directing the Unseen Energy Around You

Energy exists all around you. It exists as the thoughts and feelings that people around you project. Energy comes from the earth itself—the land, trees, and animals all emit energy. Each place on earth has a different energy, each neighborhood, each community. High altitudes have different energy than low altitudes; cities have different energy than small towns. Everything is alive in your universe and emits energy, which you can learn to sense.

You are a magnificent energy-sensing device. You can sense energy in many ways, with touch, sight, hearing, smell, feelings, thoughts and physical sensations. You can sense the universe in ways that will give you much valuable information, tuning into people's energy on a physical, emotional, or mental level by simply practicing. You can learn to tune into anyone, physically present or not. You can pick up people's thought images, their inner beliefs, and even their cries for help. Be aware that you cannot violate people's privacy in areas that their souls do not wish to reveal, however, for the soul is able to veil from anyone what it does not want to expose.

You can become aware of other people's thoughts and emotions, and even of future events, to a degree you never dreamed possible if you want to do so. To sense what is going on around you in a way that allows you to interpret and use the information, you need certain attitudes and skills, all of which can be learned easily if you are willing to pay attention and practice.

*The more you can become aware
of other people's energy,
the more aware you can become
of your own inner guidance.*

The more you can sense energy, the more you can hear your inner guidance and your higher wisdom. The next step is to become aware of what other people are sending you, of the future you are setting up for yourself, and learn to see how your energy is affecting others.

You are constantly sending thoughts and pictures to other people. It is important to become consciously aware of the images you are sending them if you want to create with awareness the reality you live in. You can send healing images to yourself with your imagination, and heal others by sending them healing images.

The first skill to develop for sensing energy is the ability to pay attention. Learn how to observe others by being silent. You know what it is like to sit back and watch. Start by observing any area about which you want more information. As you think intently about something, you will begin to receive guidance, ideas, and new thoughts about the issue.

After you stop and pay attention, the next step is to assume an attitude of confidence, and trust the information you are receiving. When you first begin to tune into your future, or into other people, you may doubt what you are receiving, and wonder if you are making it up. The doubt can be a friend if it keeps pushing you to be more accurate and precise in what you sense, as long as it does not stop you from continuing. Begin by believing in what you are sensing.

As you sit quietly and ask to see what lies ahead for you in a certain area of your life, thinking of a decision you want to make or a path you want more information about, bits and pieces of information will begin coming to you. Your intent to know the future sends your mind out to that future time, and it will bring data back to you. Sometimes information comes as a vague feeling, such as a feeling of joy or discomfort. Do not hold expectations of what you will experience. It is also important not to judge your initial attempts but to simply let any impressions come in.

A writer who is opening the flow of creativity must temporarily suspend judgment. Any creative person must suspend his judgmental, critical part during the time new information is coming through. Later, this part will be valuable in refining the information, but initially it is better to simply remain open. Likewise, when you first begin to receive impressions, suspend your judgment. Do not be critical, asking, "Is this right or is this wrong? Am I just making this up?" for that will stop the impressions from coming in. Let the impressions continue to flow. You may even want to jot them down, for you will discover later that what seems obvious and simple as it comes through often seems profound later on. When you do not write down impressions, you forget them. When you record your impressions, you get feedback.

Feedback is a very important part of your reality. In your world, actions create reactions, and it is important to be able to observe what reactions your actions cause. If you have been tuning into energy and you are beginning to get data, feelings and thoughts back, record them. Several months from now, you will probably be amazed to see the way these impressions connect with your decisions and what actually happens. It is a good way to open your awareness.

You can sense energy
to the degree your heart
is open and loving.

As you tune into others, open your heart, and embrace them with a thought of love, not criticism. Imagine an unloving, critical person tuning into someone's energy. The other person would not open (even subconsciously or on an energy level) to reveal any information, for that critical energy would feel like an intrusion. Then imagine a gentle, caring, and loving soul seeking information. The other person would open to that warmth and bask in that love. As you start to sense energy, you will discover not only the pain and confusion in others, but also different reality systems that may not fit into your own. If you approach people with compassion and tolerance, you will be able to gather much more useful data. Many people are very aware of energy, and yet when they sense something that does not fit with their known reality, with life the way they believe it to be, they tune it out. You will need to be willing to see that many people think differently and believe in different things than you without making them wrong, if you want to accurately perceive their energy.

Tolerance means you can accept many different viewpoints and love people for who they are. If you are willing to be tolerant, you can embark on an enormous adventure. Each person has a unique way of looking at the world. If you can discover what is unique, is free, open, and loving about everyone you know and meet, you will discover new ways that you yourself may become more free, open and loving. It is fascinating to discover the ways people perceive the world. As you open to many beliefs, you will become more fluid and less rigid yourself. To grow lighter yourself, be flexible and adopt whatever viewpoints are appropriate to the outcomes you desire. Most people are fixed within their own being. They have been taught the world operates in a certain way, and that is how they see it. This inflexibility leaves them with fewer and fewer areas of freedom and choice. You have seen people who are stuck in certain ruts. They are unwilling to change even though their lives don't work for them.

These people may be very unaware of other people's energy. They see everything in the world, not as they affect it, but as it affects them. They look at the world as if it revolves around them. Because they view the world this way, they often feel powerless to change things to achieve the results they want. Because they assume they are the center of the universe, they are usually unaware of other people's feelings and what reactions they are creating by their actions and deeds. If you want to direct the energy in your life, if you want to see clearly the world you live in, you will need to be willing to see life from other people's perspectives, which may be quite different from your own. As you do so, remain open and nonjudgmental, keeping a sense of discovery, love, and adventure.

*Your imagination
is a most powerful
energy-sensing tool.*

Another faculty you can use to sense energy is your imagination. You have been given an imagination to create things. Unbounded by belief structures, it is one of your most powerful energy-sensing devices. As you imagine, so do you connect with higher and finer energies. Imagination is not bound by time and space; it is not bound by your physical body. When you make things up, you often do it with a sense of joy and play, in a state of relaxation. This is a highly intuitive state.

Imagination can also be used to create fear, such as imagining your loved one with another lover, worrying about losing a job, or being afraid of catching someone's illness; but it is better to use your imagination to pretend that you know what action to take, or to create pictures of people loving you, or to imagine yourself healthy and well. When you come from the lighter energy of playfulness, when there is less heaviness or seriousness around the outcome, you are often more accurate in what you sense. If you want to sense energy, sit quietly and pretend that you can do so. If you do not know how to do something, pretend that you do, for the subconscious does not know the difference between pretending and what is truly happening. The subconscious accepts whatever you pretend is real and will use it to create your outer reality. I tell people to "magnetize your goal to you" and they tell me they do not know how. I tell them to *pretend* they know how—and it works!

As you sit, pretend that you know what someone is thinking. Imagine that you do know which decision you are going to make. Use your abilities to draw in creative ideas, and to imagine possible outcomes as tools for sensing energy and traveling into the future.

Focusing speeds up time and directs energy.

Focusing is like having a laser beam compared to an overhead light. Use your abilities of focus and concentration to sense energy. Focus is the ability to concentrate on one idea to the exclusion of all others. If you want to find information, it is important to focus upon it. The degree of focus you put on it will determine how fast you gain the knowledge you seek. Focus takes you directly to what you seek. As you concentrate on something, thinking of it to the exclusion of all else, you are directing your mind like a laser beam. When your mind is thus directed, you cannot be affected by the other energies in the universe; you are protected in that sense, and what you are focusing on becomes clear. Imagine that focus is like a beam of energy that goes out into the future, into another person, into whatever you want answers about, and lights up that area. It is like a beam of energy that goes out from you and sets up, like a telegraph wire, a way for energy and knowledge to come back. If there is anything you want to become aware of, focus upon it, for whatever you turn your attention to you will create.

As you become aware of energy, you will want to determine if it is charging or draining you. You have the ability to determine that by monitoring your energy. If you are paying attention to a certain situation and feeling drained, acknowledge your ability to know and sense truth. If you are involved in any situation, you know if you are being drained by it or charged. Become even more aware of those things that charge you, for where you turn your attention you begin to attract more of the same.

If you are in a difficult situation,
broadcast love.
Love heals and protects you.

Notice that the situations, people, or thoughts that charge you are those that operate in a positive framework, those that encourage your growth and expand your heart. Life seeks energy, awareness, and love. Every situation teaches you more about who you are. If you are in a difficult situation, one that is causing you trouble or draining your energy, begin to broadcast love, for the broadcast of love will assist you in not being drained. As love goes out, it protects the sender and stops any drain of energy.

Before you sense energy, balance and center yourself. This means putting your body in a relaxed, calm state, and quieting your emotions. You will need to learn self-monitoring techniques. As you send out your mind to other people, notice if your pulse rate increases, if you feel tense, if your body changes. All of these are ways in which you sense energy. As you tune into another person, notice what is on your mind, for the more closely you can monitor yourself, the more you can gather data and information. If you are thinking of someone and you find yourself feeling suddenly worried about your finances, you are picking up the other person's worry if you were not worrying about finances before you thought of him.

If you are trying to look into the future, to see the outcome of something, often the information will come back not through your mind, but through your body. You may be trying to decide upon a path, and as you think of one choice you notice your breathing has grown shallow, your body is somewhat closed, and that you feel discomfort in your stomach. These are signs from the future you are sensing that are telling you about this path. If when you think of a certain path, you feel heavy inside, your body is telling you there is a better way to do it. Keep imagining possible futures, varying slightly the things you are thinking about doing, until you have a light and joyful feeling. If none of them gives you a light feeling, try out some new alternatives. Learn to monitor yourself, for you are an energy-sensing device, and as you monitor yourself, you begin to find the clues and the answers that are there.

Interpreting what you have received is the next step. After you have brought all the information in, even recorded it, sit and read or review it. You may find many doubts coming up; it is important at this time that you do not let them stop you. Thank them and let them go. As you open to your abilities to read the energy around you, you may discover that there is a voice within that does not believe what you are sensing. It is true for almost everyone, so do not fault yourself if you discover this to be so. As long as your heart is open, as long as you are not coming from ego, personal gain, manipulation or any of those energies you know are not high, you can trust what you are sensing. Sometimes the information you gather may seem to serve the ego. If it does, you must examine it closely, using

both your mind and your ability to sense energy. If it is
something you have been wanting to happen, and you are
very involved emotionally, then your ability to sense clearly may be impaired. The clearest information comes when
the emotions are calm, when there is no personal gain and
you are simply seeking information to assist or help
another. As you practice, however, you can still bring in
valuable information about yourself, even when you are
feeling emotional about an issue.

Say you have a friend who is in trouble. You sit quietly
one day, using all of the techniques I have mentioned, sensing your friend's energy. You begin to see life through his
or her eyes. You see that there are certain beliefs that are
not working and that there is pain inside. You see this
without any judgment, with only a sense of great love and
concern. As you sense this energy, there is no personal gain
for you, there is no sense of manipulation, only a true and
burning desire to help. Trust the information that comes
in. Ask for your higher self to be with you, and for the
higher forces of the universe to assist you. Request that
you become a channel for that higher information, and
open to the information coming to you. If your purpose
and intent is to create more light in your life and others',
then what you receive will help you in doing so. If you act
in this manner, from the heart, with a sense of service,
your ability to sense energy will increase rapidly, and there
are no doors that will not open to you.

*Spend time thinking of
what you want rather
than what you don't want.*

The less time you spend sending out pictures of what
you want, the more your space will be filled with other

people's visions of what they want you to do, or with lower or less evolved images that come from your old patterns. You will be living those pictures rather than having what you want. The world of images is the source of power in your physical world. Imagining what you want is like creating a model before you build the real thing. The images direct the energy in your body. If there is a situation in your life you would like resolved, you can always ask for images and symbols that will help you. Often, when you receive images and pictures, such as through your dreams, you want to find logical explanations and know the meaning of the symbols. It is not necessary to know what they mean to be healed by them.

You can heal other people by sending them symbols and images. You can heal a situation by envisioning and symbolizing it as easily as you can heal it with words. Symbols are, in fact, more direct and more healing than words, for they are not connected to your belief systems. Think of a situation in your life right now, something you would like an answer to, and ask for a healing image. See if you can get an image of the other person involved, or the entire situation. If you have someone in your life who is causing you trouble, tying up your time and energy, try to see him or her symbolically. He may appear to be coming at you with a battering ram, and you might see yourself as a wall that constantly gives into his force. You could work with the situation by changing and healing the symbols, perhaps imagining the battering ram changing into a tiny piece of cardboard and your wall becoming flexible like rubber. You absolutely can shift energy by playing with symbols, and you can heal any situation in this way.

There are currents of energy that circle the planet and you can tap into them anytime you want. If you want physical energy, you can breathe deeply and imagine that you are connected to the flow of all the people who have an abundance of vitality. At any one time there are millions of people focused on certain ideas. There are photographers, writers, meditators, spiritual people, to name a few, and you can use their energy broadcast to increase or bring into yourself whatever you want. Simply close your eyes and tune in (even if it is just with your imagination) to all those people who are doing the same thing you are. Tune into their flow of high, successful energy. Through your breathing, you can draw in your global connection to other people or to the assistance and guidance from the higher forces of the universe.

Any energy you want exists in the world. If you want more love, you can breathe in the love that is there, circling the planet. Sooner or later it will be there in your physical reality. If you are working on a project and find difficulties in completing it, you can tune into all the people out there who are successfully completing their projects. You can be a healing influence in everything you do. Use your ability to sense and tune into energy to evolve yourself and others; it is a skill you can develop that will help evolve you rapidly.

PLAYSHEET

1 | Take one person you know and describe the person's
life as he or she sees it.

Christine. ~~Her~~ Life is difficult & taken on
many hardships. Life is a gift, nurturing,
yet very difficult to be abundant.
Life can be very happy yet lonely
afraid, critical, & bitter.

2 | How could you help and support this person in his or
her growth? Make a picture in your mind of what you
could do to assist him or her.

Being her friend & sending her
positive thoughts & encouragement.
Love. I imagine her being
cradled & supported by the great
earth mother & accepting love
free from judgment & being full
of joy & peace.

3 | Take a situation in your life you would like to know the future of. Now pretend that you are five years in the future and looking back at today. What does this self have to tell you about what will happen? Let your imagination run free and have fun with this. Make up what will happen. (You might want to keep this somewhere to look at later.)

- I want to be completely self employed w/ all my own contracts
- none

My self tells me that it will totally happen + will be well deserved.

All I need is patience & good attitude.

IV

Sensing Energy
in Others

Many of you are developing the ability to maintain your sense of self and steer clear of the mass or group thinking that does not fit you. Energy is like a current. Often it flows around and past you. It can be thought of as an aroma drifting around, affecting or not affecting you depending upon how you choose to react to it and how aware you are of it. The more aware you are of yourself, the less outside influences can affect you. The less aware you are of yourself and the less conscious attention you pay to who you are, the more energy can affect you.

All of you are aware of your feelings and thoughts to one degree or another. You certainly know when you feel happy or depressed; you know whether your thoughts are negative or positive. You can learn to go deeper, becoming aware of the subtle currents and flows of energy and how they affect you. You can become an observer of the energy around you, directing it rather than reacting to it.

For a moment, think back on your day. What feelings did you have today? Can you remember how you felt when you were with various people? You probably experienced many different emotions ranging from high, happy, positive thoughts and experiences to feelings of anger, frustration, anxiety, or depression. Some of your feelings were reactions to the people you were with.

People constantly broadcast their energy. Just as people have their own personal body chemistry, so do they have their own unique energy broadcast. Energy can be equated to a code. Just as there are no two snowflakes alike, there are no two codes alike. Each person you are with affects you somewhat differently.

Become aware of your body when you are with a particular person. Are you hunched over, or are you straight? Are your arms folded in front of you, or are your arms in back of you, leaving your heart open? Are your shoulders back or forward? Are you leaning forward or backward from the waist, or are you straight up and down? Your body will always give you clues about how you are handling people.

A*wareness of your body,*
thoughts, and emotions
allows you to discover
the effect other people
have on you.

Tomorrow, or for the next week, notice how you feel with each person you come in contact with. Pay attention to your emotions. You may not feel as if you are being affected by them until you take a deeper look at what is happening to you. When you are with one person you may suddenly start worrying about finances, although ten minutes earlier you felt fine about money. You have brought his energy into yourself.

If you are leaning forward, you are giving away your energy and trying to push in on other people's space. If you are leaning way back, you are avoiding their energy, and they are coming at you too strongly. When you are sitting or standing straight, with your shoulders square, you are most in your power, for that is definitely a position of balance and centeredness which allows you to control the energy around you. With both feet flat on the floor, your body breathing rhythmically and your shoulders square, you can bring in your higher self.

You will also become more aware of the effect people have on you by looking at your thoughts. Be aware of what issues you begin thinking of when you are around various people. When you are with one person you may find yourself constantly thinking of love, transformation and the beauty of the universe. When you are with another, you may find yourself thinking how hard things are, how difficult your life is, how much work you have ahead of you. Monitor your thinking when you are with people and when you spend time alone. Unless you know how you think when you are alone, you will not be able to recognize the effect other people have on your thoughts.

Look out for the effect others have on your emotions too. You may feel suddenly tired, or happy and charged with energy, or drained, depressed, anxious or angry. Pay attention to the differences. Learn how to be not drained but activated and charged by your connections with people. The first step is to become aware of when someone's presence leaves you drained, even in a very subtle way. Many of you make yourself wrong when you feel depleted by people. You say, "I am not trying hard enough to please them." Or, "Maybe I didn't say the right thing." "Maybe I didn't get my point across." "Maybe I wasn't good enough, or loving enough." You then look for ways in which *you* might have been wrong, and step up your efforts to please the other person.

Do not make
the other person, or yourself,
wrong.

You cannot have a healing connection if you see yourself as wrong or lacking. If you are feeling bad about a relationship, say to yourself, "I am perfect as I am." Then go deeper into yourself. Monitor your energy when you are speaking to that person. Be aware of your feelings, thoughts, and body. Constantly check in with yourself and ask, "Do I feel good? Do I feel high, or am I feeling inadequate?" There is absolutely no reason to be around anyone who makes you feel bad about yourself.

As you deepen your awareness of the energy dynamics of a situation, you can pick up messages from the interaction that will tell you more about yourself. For instance, suppose you are talking to someone and it seems he only wants to talk about himself and does not want to hear about you. You feel depreciated and angry, or maybe you feel he doesn't value you. As you look into yourself, you may realize that *you* don't listen to or value your feelings, or that *you* have many inner messages you aren't paying attention to. Every interaction can tell you something about yourself. As you heal and change the drama within yourself, you will find that you do not attract those types of interactions anymore.

Unless you are involved in healing, don't put yourself around anyone who wants to drain or use your energy. When you heal people, you direct the energy, and they cannot make you feel depleted. (Unless you take in their energy or they are resisting your healing.) There is no reason to put yourself in a situation where you feel depreciated, unloved or undervalued.

Why do you allow yourself to be in situations throughout the day, even minor ones with store clerks, customers, or telephone calls, in which you are made to feel depreciated? It is because of a belief many of you picked up from your culture that you do not have the right to choose whom you are around. You may feel you owe your time and energy to others, or that you are obligated to give them attention if they want to be a part of your life. Some of you believe you must be loving, supportive, and caring to everyone. Loving someone does not mean making their feelings more important than your own. If you study the lives of highly evolved beings, you will see that there are many ways to be loving to others, including being blunt and not tolerating petty behavior, although speaking bluntly is done with compassion and love.

Being committed to your higher purpose and loving to yourself is the first priority. In your day-to-day contacts, know that you do not owe anyone your time or energy. They are the greatest gifts you have been given, and how you use them will determine how much you will evolve in this lifetime.

When you are feeling depreciated, angry, or drained, it is a sign that other people are not open to your energy.

They may be receiving it in a way that is not healing, perhaps to feed their ego. They may be blocking you and not wanting your energy. When you notice that you are feeling depleted in any way, if you are leaning forward, trying to reach others, begging for their attention, or feeling drained, unappreciated, unacknowledged or unsupported, it is time to ask why you remain in that situation.

When you feel depreciated or drained by a stranger for no apparent reason, you are suffering from what has been called a "psychic whack." These connections are messages from the universe telling you to pay attention to what you are doing to yourself, to look at ways you may be giving away your energy to those who cannot receive it. I call them reminders. The minute you find yourself being whacked, or depreciated, by someone you will probably not see again, or only know as a distant contact, look more closely at the relationships you have with friends and loved ones. You may be depreciating yourself in some way. If the universe cannot reach you with its messages about those close relationships, it will send a stranger to you to catch your attention. It is only a reminder that there is some area in your life in which you are undervaluing yourself. Thank the person for that reminder, and then begin to look more closely at your relationships. Ask, "Where am I giving out my energy and not having it returned?"

Most of you desire to love and heal and help the people you know, and want intimate loving connections with others. Loving relationships come when the people you love and assist are open to receiving. Imagine you had neighbors you wanted to give to, so you constantly sent them gifts. They, on the other hand, felt irritated, and resented the feeling that you were putting them under obligation when they did not have the time or desire to return your gifts. You would begin feeling unappreciated, wondering why they did not thank you or give back to you. You would question why you did not feel good even though you were generous and giving. As you can see, there are many times in which it is not appropriate to give to others. They might begin to resent you because they have not asked for your gift of love and healing.

If you want a healing connection with others, know how much to give, and how much to receive.

It is important to know how much you are capable of receiving, for many of you are not very open to accepting anything, although you love to give to others. If you feel that others do not appreciate what you give them, it is time to take a look at how open you are to receiving from others.

All of you have had the experience of not being appreciated. Ask yourself, "Was I trying to give more than the other person was capable of taking in?" That is another way your friends can drain you.

People who are in the healing professions can be drained and feel depreciated, can experience burnout, when their gift of energy is not flowing both ways. There is nothing more energizing to both the healer and the receiver than a two-way flow of love. Then healing can actually be seen, and growth occurs. The healer is just as charged by the person receiving energy as the person receiving it is invigorated by the healer. When you are in a healing role with people, you can be drained if they cannot receive, and they can be drained if you give more than they can receive.

Negative emotions such as obligation, anger, or resentment, always come up when your energy is being drained. If you monitor yourself, by checking in on your thoughts, feelings, and body, you will know if the energy exchange is equal. If you find that you are being depleted, and do not like how you feel, what action can you take? First, know that you absolutely can control your thoughts, emotions, and physical body reactions. You can go inside and ask the universe and your spirit to help you see clearly, to speak to you of your lessons.

Many of you are in situations in which you feel the energy exchange is not equal. Suppose someone is constantly borrowing money from you and not paying you back. The more you try to get repaid, with no results, the angrier you get. You can go within and ask, "Is it symbolic of my giving away my energy and not opening to receive it back?" You can find many messages about how your energy flows by paying attention to those areas in which you feel drained, and you can reframe those messages into challenges and lessons. If you have a belief that says you do not deserve to have all that you want, affirm to yourself that you *can* have relationships that are healing for both you and others.

All of you have reservations about the energy you sense. You may think, "Am I really sensing this energy, am I really feeling depreciated and drained, or am I just tired today and imagining it?" Do not worry about your doubts. They can also represent your strong side which keeps you from being too pulled by the various currents of energy around you. The key is learning to turn your doubts into friends. Sometimes you will hear a voice of disbelief speaking up about certain things in your life. It says, "Maybe it will never work. Maybe it's all a pipe dream. Maybe I'll never get what I want. Maybe I'm not right." That little voice of uncertainty can be so big. Listen to it. Talk to it. For there is always valuable information coming from that voice. What could be the message, the benefit of that voice of doubt? Many of you respond to the voice by saying, "No, I will not be discouraged. I will keep the faith. I will keep my vision. I'm going to try anyway." When you fight the voice of skepticism, it has already accomplished its goal, which was to bring out your strong side and strengthen it.

Sometimes the doubts can seem almost overwhelming, and your powerful voice must be even louder to be heard. When you feel yourself going into doubt, questioning your power, your interpretation of things, your path, talk to that voice and ask it what it is trying to tell you. Ask what gift it is giving you. The sooner you acknowledge that there is a gift in that voice of uncertainty, the more quickly it will be quiet and assist you in having what you want.

The other message from the voice of doubt is a challenge to see how much you believe in yourself. When you wonder if you really feel drained or not, your lesson is to believe in your feelings. If you feel even the slightest bit drained, begin to look at the energy dynamics between you and the person you are with. Trust that you would not feel drained unless you really were being drained.

Emotions can lead you to answers but can also block a clear connection to your intuition when you are sensing energy. What do emotions do, and why do you have them?

Emotions help you create reality.

When you believe in something, love, desire, and want it, you can create it more quickly. Love your emotions, but do not let them deplete your energy. And don't allow the

emotions of others to drain you either. The emotions of
other people can exhaust or capture your energy only to
the degree to which you allow those same feelings within
to capture you. No one can harm you with his powerful,
intense or negative emotions, unless you have those same
emotions. Other people's feelings awaken within you your
matching emotions, through the principle of resonance. As
you calm your own emotions, you will be able to handle
other people's strong emotions.

How do you calm your emotions? Listen to the slightly
negative feelings within you before they create a crisis.
Your higher self is always speaking to you through your
emotions, leading you this way or that. If you do not listen
at the lower level of intensity, your emotions will grow
stronger. It is the same when you listen to other people. If
you do not pay attention when you are being slightly
depreciated by people, they may continue to deplete and
drain your energy until you "get it." They may exhaust
you more and more until you stop them either by ter-
minating the relationship, or by speaking to them of what
you want.

When you begin to notice situations that are undervaluing you, or demanding too much from you, clear the
negative energy. First, remain straight and strong and
centered in your body; do not lean forward or backward.
When you are with people who drain you, learn to put
your feelings into words, even if just to yourself.

Putting your feelings into words is very powerful in
cleansing other people's energy from your space. Do not
express anger to other people, but do get it out of your
system. Say it into a tape recorder, or into a video camera,
or write it down. Any process that brings it out of your
body is a process of healing and cleansing yourself of the
energy you have taken on from other people.

Emotions can block the clear sensing of energy. When you are highly emotional about an issue, it is much more difficult to see your higher path. Before asking the Universe for answers, be sure to find a peaceful, quiet space within yourself for the answers to flow into.

Many of you, when you listen to others, are constantly chattering in your mind, thinking of answers you will give, thinking of things to say back. I call it doing rather than being. Doing is when your mind is constantly busy, when you are within yourself, carrying on an inner dialogue. Being is when you are very silent, listening with intent and focus to what others are saying.

Listen with a silent mind.
You can then direct
the flow of energy
between yourself and others.

The busier your mind is, the more you are apt to be unconsciously affected by energy. The more silent your inner dialogue when you are listening to another, the more you can direct the outcome, and be aware of your body and emotions in the interaction. When you are with others, practice being. Practice not trying to do anything, think of anything, or respond to anything. Simply become aware of the sounds, the smells, the room, the energy interaction at a level beyond words. Monitor how you feel and observe what is being said. You will find a wealth of information flowing into you.

You may be surprised as you begin seeing the kind of relationships you have been having, the connections you thought were high and healing but were not. You may, for the first time, truly see the energy others are giving or not giving you.

Be aware of the world you exist in. Be aware of the messages that are constantly being sent to you by the loving, higher forces of the universe, and most of all, pay attention to yourself.

PLAYSHEET

1 | Sit quietly and relax your body. Tune into your own energy, your body, emotions, and mind to get a sense of your reality. Then, think of someone you know. Send your mind out gently, open your heart, and listen quietly while any images, pictures, or feelings come back. Notice the difference between your feelings and theirs. Notice any changes in your body or emotions or thoughts, then come back into your own reality. Record any impressions you received.

2 | Share with this person your experience, giving him or her any positive information or loving insights you received. Get feedback, for through feedback you become able to more and more accurately interpret what you receive.

V

Who am I?

The question of "Who am I?" is important, for without knowing who you are, you cannot clearly sense or interpret the energy around you.

All of you have a sense of who you are; you have observed yourselves in many different situations, and you know how you react, how you use your time, etc. Most of you also have a vision of who you wish you were—how you would like your body to look, how you would like to use your time, how much money you want to make, what exercise you should get and what food you think you should eat. We will speak later of all those images and pictures you carry around about who you think you should be, that vision of who you want to be.

To know who you are, you need to find the stillness of your mind. I have spoken of stillness and the screen which is created through relaxation and visualization. Knowing who you are involves time alone, quiet and reflective time in which you can listen to your thoughts, and reflect upon the day and yourself.

To know who you are means making a commitment to yourself. What is a commitment to yourself? Some of you think it means using your will power to force yourself to live that vision of who you think you should be. You may feel that once you have decided to do something, you must stand inflexibly by that decision.

Making a commitment to yourself means listening to your feelings from moment to moment and acting on what is right for you in present time.

Almost all of the resolutions you make about how you will act involve projecting your present-time self into a future time. That means making decisions for a time that has not yet arrived. Making a commitment to yourself is being in present time, acknowledging that you have enough sense of self to do what is right at this moment. It is trusting yourself, knowing you do not have to wake up and tell yourself how you will be, how you will handle things; you do not have to worry about three weeks from today or a year from now. It is knowing that you will not be the same person at that future time, that you will be wiser and more evolved. It is important to plan and visualize what you want for the future, but then relax and trust your future self.

Making a commitment to yourself is knowing what is appropriate at the present time. To do so you must know your feelings. You may say, "I know how I feel," yet many of you do not know how you feel, and even more of you do not back your feelings with words or actions. For instance, if someone asks you to do him a favor, you may say, "That is not something I want to do, but I should do it." And you do it anyway, going against your feelings. When you make a pledge to honor yourself, others may call you selfish. You may have programming that says it is wrong to be selfish, that you owe something or are obligated in some way to others. You cannot sense energy clearly, you cannot be powerful and direct energy, unless your first commitment is to yourself. If you do not make your life, thoughts, goals, and time a priority, you will be lost in the currents of other people's desires and expectations. Whatever comes your way, such as a person, a project, or an event, will constantly knock you back and forth like a small dingy on an ocean of huge waves. If you do know who you are, make your life a priority, acknowledge your feelings and act upon them, you can then have a strong vessel sailing calm waters, in a direction you have chosen.

K*now when to pay attention to your own needs and when to be selfless.*

While it is important to be centered on yourself and know who you are, making your life a priority, it is also important to be aware of your affect on other people. You are more powerful when you can understand the effect your actions have on others, and then choose what actions you want to take. Some people worry that if they do what is right for themselves they will be acting in a selfish way. When you honor your higher path and self, you always honor the higher path and self of others, even if it does not seem so at the time. It is also important to know when to be selfless—when to flow with things and not come from the demands of your own ego. The best guidelines I can give are to be selfless when it comes to the unimportant things—what table you get at a restaurant, what movie you go to, and let the small things slide by. When it comes to following your higher vision, to doing those things that serve mankind, then that is the time to take a stand (a very compassionate and gentle one, however). It is important to be selfless when you are a part of a larger group, working toward community goals, if those goals are part of your higher purpose and there is a sense of joy in that service and selflessness. If selflessness comes from guilt, pressure, or a "have to" attitude, then it is not appropriate.

Most of you are wrapped up in your own lives. You are so concerned with your impact on other people, wondering, "What will so-and-so think when I tell her what I am doing?" that you often do not see who you are except from a limited perspective. There are many ways to exit your body and change your perspective, to see yourself in a new light. One is to put yourself in other people's shoes, look at them not through your own judgments and beliefs, but through their beliefs and perspective. Many of you constantly feel you are actors on a stage, with everybody watching and judging you. But it is only you that has put yourself on a stage, watching, observing and judging. When you do this, you also begin to feel responsible for other people—if they feel bad then you may feel you caused it.

D*o not feel responsible for everyone's happiness. Only they can choose it, you cannot choose it for them.*

You have seen small children who feel they caused their parents' divorce, because in their young eyes every-thing that happens appears to be something they caused. If you want to get a new perspective of who you are, see yourself through the eyes of another person. Put yourself in the other person's shoes. Think of his or her challenges, attitudes, abundance or lack of it, and let the images flow. You have just left your body and your reality, and become a part of another's energy system. You will understand another person's actions and behavior by stepping outside of your life and viewpoint, and you will also be able to sense yourself more clearly. Look at your life through his or her eyes. You can begin tomorrow with all the people you come in contact with. You can look at the reality they are living in, the stress they are under, the kinds of thoughts that go on in their minds, and what their lessons are right now. With this understanding, you can interact with them in a way that is healing to you and them. Make this process a habitual one, something you do without trying or thinking. Then, when you are worried about others, concerned with what they think of you, or what is hap-pening to them, you will be able to use the same process to sense their energy.

One of the biggest blind spots in sensing energy is being too aware of yourself, existing too much on the cen-ter stage of your own life. You are blocked from sensing other people's realities when you are more concerned with what others think about you than with what you can do to heal and assist them (which, of course, heals and assists *you*). As we speak of moving upward to higher energy lev-els, we are speaking of healing others, and making every contact you have throughout the day a healing one.

You cannot become more sensitive to energy until you can handle it in a healing way. The universe would not allow you to experience that much energy if you did not know how to handle it. The more you can work with the energy you sense in a way that heals you and the other person, the more you will be able to sense and know the energies that exist around you.

What is a healing contact? How do you make every connection a healing one? The first step toward healing connections is to forgive people as you come in contact with them. First, become aware of any resentment you may have had or have now towards them, any feelings of superiority or inferiority, any grudge, any negative thoughts you have sent to them (even if it is only a picture that something about them is not up to your standards). To heal, feel a sense of forgiveness for yourself for anything you have sent them on a thought or emotional level that has not assisted them in their growth. Ask yourself how you can assist them in their spiritual unfoldment. What communication could you give that would serve them? To find an answer you must leave your body and become a part of their reality. How can you appreciate them, acknowledge and thank them? Those questions and thoughts will take you outside the narrow focus of your personality.

Give to others what you want to receive—love, support, appreciation, healing, and acknowledgment—and you will get it back.

Wondering, "How can *I* be acknowledged, have more support, or get what *I* want?" blocks your clear sensing of energy. Giving opens your ability to see others and their systems of reality, and it most definitely enables you to see yourself in a higher and more loving way.

You will automatically begin forgiving, supporting, acknowledging and appreciating yourself when you do so for others. Healing others is not just a gift you are giving to the world. It is also a gift to yourself.

All of you can learn to be aware of your own energy by seeing other people's energy. The more accurately you perceive energy in other people, the more precisely you will be able to sense it in yourself. This is true not only of positive energy but also of fear and dark energy. When you judge others, you feel your own shadow and bring into yourself any negative energy you are judging. To see energy clearly is to leave behind right-wrong judgments. Challenge yourself to let go of a right-wrong framework. When you observe a quality or characteristic in others that you do not like, see if you can find how it fits into their life. Look at how that particular trait works for them, what that quality does for them. Leaving behind judgment frees you from being affected by other people's energy.

What is fear? What is that shadow area? Until it is looked at, fear often exists as a feeling of heaviness, worry or concern. There are moments when you feel light and joyful and there are moments when you do not. Those heavier moments are often an indication of fear. The higher you go the more you will be releasing fear.

*To dissolve fear,
turn and look directly at it,
for what you face dissolves
in the light of consciousness.*

Fear at the lower levels exists as heavy emotions, as a weight, a feeling of tension in the body. It can be a feeling of rushing around, trying to hide under the guise of productivity, doing rather than being.

When you feel heavy or dark, ask the fear to come into your consciousness. Anything you turn your back on will grow and become worse. When you are willing to stand and face what you fear, the universe will assist you in releasing and healing it. Many of you fear that you are alone; you believe that you must handle everything yourself. You may feel the great weight of responsibility, yet the universe is full of friends, healers, and help. The more you begin to heal those you contact, the more healing will come back to you. Receiving and giving healing is the pathway into higher energy.

Fear can often be faced and transformed by breathing relaxation into the body. It also can be handled by action. When you are sensing negative energy in another, a feeling you do not like, do not run and hide from it. First, suspend your judgment and then ask the universe for guidance about what action (if any) you can take. The universe will always send you assistance when you ask for it. It may come through your thoughts as insights or revelations; it may come through something you see or read; or it may come through something you hear. When you feel any negativity in another, you can stop it from affecting you by asking how you can heal and support them in their growth. You will find that they will look for ways to do the same for you. If they cannot match you in your healing and loving energy, they will leave your life, or you will find yourself not creating as many opportunities to be with them.

What is the fear of sensing energy, what is the fear of finding negative energy in others? Is it a fear that they can harm you? Is it a belief that others can bring you down or make you less? When you become consciously aware of your fear of negative energy, when you are in touch with how you think negative energy can harm you, then you have a basis to begin working with it. Only by facing and acknowledging your fear of negative energy can you transmute it into harmless energy. Again, positive healing energy is always more powerful than negative energy.

Fear can be generated in any area where your images of who you are now and who you want to be do not match. Why do you fear who you are not? Do you feel you are a disappointment to yourself, that you have let yourself down?

Love *and accept who you are,
not who you will be or should be.*

If you love yourself for who you are, you are living in present time which is the gateway to personal power. If you love only who you will be, then you are out of your body, living in a future you cannot affect (until it becomes present time and you can act). Look at who you are, compare it to who you want to be, and ask yourself why they do not match. Ask, "Is what I want to be really appropriate to who I am, or is it something I was told I should be?" The more you can clear yourself of other people's programs, expectations, and pictures of you, the more powerful you will become. Many of those future pictures involve meeting unrealistic or inappropriate standards given to you by others. Many of those ideals represent beliefs of others that you try to fit onto yourself. Look clearly at your expectations of yourself, especially those you constantly fail to meet. They can be indicators of areas in which who you want to be is not fitting with your true needs. The pain you feel at the difference, the feelings of heaviness, fear, or darkness, only exist because you are trying to "wear" energy that does not belong to you.

Knowing who you are requires reflective time, quiet time. Time alone is some of the most important time you can create. I am not speaking of time in which you are frantically thinking of something, but peaceful time in which you are not thinking of anything. The stillness of the mind creates space for ideas to come into your reality and be born. Inspiration is born in stillness. It may be a week or more before a new idea comes into your conscious awareness. But do not let the time delay keep you from seeing the connection between quiet time and the creativity that comes later.

Being alone, sitting quietly, allowing yourself to rest physically, emotionally, and mentally will give you an increasingly clear sense of self. In those still times you are not playing out any role or any identity, and your soul can speak to you more clearly. You have the clearest sense of your own energy when you are not around others, when you are alone. Some of you are around others all the time, and when you finally find yourself alone you create a million things to do—anything to keep from thinking, reflecting and being quiet. You have been taught that productivity and creating things you can see, touch, or hear is more valuable than quiet time. However, reflective time is the source of energy revitalization, of clear seeing, of ideas and inspiration. Begin valuing any time you can create to sit or lie and be quiet. Practice not thinking of anything, for stillness is the doorway to sensing energy and to opening your intuition. It is also the highest and most effective form of self-healing that you will find.

PLAYSHEET

1 | Think of an upcoming meeting with a friend or loved one.

2 | What is the higher purpose of your meeting? It could be to encourage or support each other or to help with a decision. Even if it is purely social, see if you can discover the higher purpose in your being together.

3 | How could you assist the other person in creating a higher vision of who they are? How could they assist you in the same way? The next time you are together, decide you will focus and act on the higher purpose of the meeting.

VI

Bringing the Unconscious into Consciousness

You have within you all the tools you need to become what you want. As you learn to sense energy, you can also evolve the energy you experience. As you become conscious of the energy around you, you can note when your energy is high, and bring it even higher. This allows you to evolve the pictures in your mind and focus your intent so that you can become clearer, go higher, and expand and evolve.

When you ask the universe for more, it is important to be open as to how it comes, for the universe will give it to you in the fastest, most efficient way possible. You may need to let go of certain attitudes or images before you can have something, so you will set up situations to release them. If you are ready to go higher, it is time to let go of any pictures about how you will get there.

You can evolve more quickly by bringing your unconscious to consciousness, for the conscious mind is the light that evolves the unconscious. You are by no means run by hidden drives or unknown programs. You have been given the ability to look inward and find answers.

To bring the unconscious to consciousness, focus on finding the light around any situation. You will find answers coming, without the need to use your mind to analyze and think. If you want an answer, imagine that you hold the situation in your hands. Imagine light coming into that image, and then release it to your higher self or to a higher being in the universe.

You are not at the mercy
of hidden drives or unknown programs.
You have the ability to look inward
and find answers.

If you seek an answer, all you need do is ask, then listen. Some things get in the way of your listening, however, and one of those is your picture of what reality is and how it operates. Another interference is a mind that chatters incessantly, one that keeps thinking when you need to rest or think in another way.

Bringing the unconscious into consciousness is the challenge of every situation you are in. If you feel that something you do not understand has happened, already you are spending much time with the intent to solve it, analyze it, and know it. You are sending a beacon of energy out into the universe. Immediately answers are being broadcast back to you. If you expect the answer to come in a certain way or be a certain answer, then it will be difficult for new and more expansive answers to come through. Take any question you want answered and stop thinking of it for a week. Once you have asked a question, it is important to let go of it. If you could take any issue and not think of it for even one day, you would find a whole new energy around the situation.

Another way of bringing the unconscious up into the known is to sit quietly with yourself and work with your images. If you are going back and forth over an issue, then neither answer is completely right. If you had the right answer, you would not be going back and forth. You can help release this situation by seeing yourself finding an answer. If you cannot see why certain things are happening to you, hold an image of yourself understanding things easily and quickly. You can go back into your memory and recall all the times you did understand events as they were happening.

Whatever is happening in your life is coming from an image you hold about yourself. The images you send out attract situations to you. These pictures are absolutely available to your conscious awareness. You can change any situation by looking at and changing your vision of yourself.

If you were to sit for a few minutes, put on peaceful music and think of nothing else except the situation at hand, you would find yourself moving through it very quickly and able to let go of it afterwards, not needing to think of it over and over. In moving to higher levels of consciousness, certain qualities must exist. One is focus. If your mind is always thinking of ten or fifteen issues, it may take weeks to move through them. If you find yourself thinking of many things and feeling pressured scattered, busy, or if you find there is not enough time, your mind is trying to handle too many things. Each moment has its highest purpose, each person you are with has his or her highest purpose. If you are ready to move into higher levels of energy you can do so by increasing the amount of time you spend there.

You can become aware, when your energy is down, of what took it there. I will tell you what things take most people's energy down: talking about mundane or negative things; reading articles in newspapers or magazines which speak of pain or struggle without a higher reason for it; not listening to the flow of your body (not resting when tired, not being active when energy is there); thinking of past times in which you were hurt; fearing the future.

You bring up your energy when you do what you feel like doing. If you set a goal to get something done, and yet find you want to do something else, you would raise your energy by getting up and doing the other thing. You may find the goal you set has changed. Or, you may find the break just what you needed to recharge your enthusiasm.

*As you focus on
what is good about people,
you enable them to achieve it.*

There are many ways to bring up your energy. Start by becoming aware of what you say to people. Are you building them up? Are you holding an ennobling vision of them? Whatever you point a finger at will grow—if you focus on people's weaknesses, emphasizing in your mind what is wrong with them, it will grow. If you have any situations in your life that are not working, the more you picture them as not working, the more you create it as so.

When two people first fall in love, they see the best in each other and hold that vision. Suddenly, they find

themselves able to accomplish new things and find old, *of yourself*
negative patterns leaving. You can greatly assist people by
holding an image ~~for~~ them of their success, joy and
abundance.

Be aware of the images
you create about yourself
when you speak to others.

Do you speak of prosperity, joy, and abundance or do
you speak of pain, problems and woes? People form images of you as you speak to them. You may think that if
you told everyone how abundant your life is when it isn't
you'd be lying—yet I will say if you tell everyone how
abundant your life is, very shortly you will be telling the
truth! Watch your words and your energy as you move
through the day. The instant you notice that your energy is
dropping in any way, that doubts are creeping into your
mind, that you are feeling bad about who you are, stop.
Take a deep breath and look inward for a higher image.
You broadcast images from moment to moment, and
people pick them up and respond to them.

If you want to know why something happened to you,
hold up the belief that you do know why. It is important to
learn forgiveness, because every time you replay a
negative memory, making yourself wrong, you are
creating it again in the future. In moments of crisis a new
self is often born, a baby self, one that has just come into
being with the crisis. Like a small child it may not have the
skills to handle things perfectly or beautifully, and yet that
self is growing every moment. It is not a gift to this new
being if you go back and send it images of its wrongness.

*You never do anything
that is not in some way
an attempt to bring more
light into your life.*

You can go back to any crisis and see that a new self, a new part of you was born. It is a stronger and clearer part, a part that is more committed to your life, your truth, your growth.

You may be setting up a crisis right now, a challenge or dilemma, to prepare for the birth of a new self. You are always going for the light. You may have interpreted what you did as not being the best you could do, so it is important to go back and change your vision, release and forgive yourself, and see what you learned. Look at what qualities the situation is developing or developed in you. It may be leading you to a deeper truth or helping you learn about what you want by experiencing what you don't want. You may be learning to see your own light and to become more powerful, assertive, and clearly focused. Whatever you think you are not, you are working on becoming. Whatever any of you are asking for right now, you will have, but it may not come in the way you expect it.

Watch the energy of everyone you meet when they speak to you. Watch their words, and if you sense your energy dropping become extra alert. Pay attention to the topic. You will find that there are things to speak of with other people that bring up your energy, and things that do not. You have the ability to change the topic into something that raises the level of the interaction. Notice what thoughts you carry around in your mind. Whatever thoughts are on your mind when you die will be those that will direct you to where you are going afterwards. Where are your thoughts during the day? How often are you thinking of your highest vision, your higher self?

To bring the subconscious
into the higher self,
look at each area of your life and ask,
"What is my highest vision?"

You may think that you need to be involved in the daily, mundane details of your life, and yet these things can get taken care of effortlessly if you are focused on your highest vision and your higher path. Look at your level of abundance, how much you let the universe give you. Is there a way to increase how much you receive? It is important to find your deeper motivation. If you want more money, why? What do you think you will get from having money that you do not have now? If you want something, what is your motivation? If you knew your motivation you would know the driving force behind everything you do. Motivation is a driving force that can bring anything you want. You may be saying "if I had this car, or that job, or a man, I would be happy." There is more here than meets the eye. If you knew your deepest motivation for having these, you could have your needs met in many ways. It may be that you want more security or delight, to feel more relaxed, or loved, or to receive more. When you are in touch with the essence of what you desire, you can have it in many ways. If you do not focus on a specific thing to bring you what you want, the universe can truly begin bringing you abundance in many ways.

When you think of issues you want to resolve you have two choices—you can ask your higher self to give you a higher vision of the issue, or you can release the issue to your higher self and ask that your higher self take care of it for you. The best solutions come from your higher self.

It is important to create new and higher images of yourself. Ask your friends to hold specific images of you, such as picturing you succeeding at something you are doing. If you do not have new pictures your mind will be much more tempted to fall back into the old ways of thinking. If you were filled with thoughts of what would be absolutely joyful in your life, such as traveling, more free time, a loving relationship, a physical body that is becoming stronger and more fit every day, you would not have time to think at the old, more painful or mundane levels.

When you evolve your images you evolve the energy you sense. You can control the energy you come in contact with. If you find people talking about you in a way that does not match your higher vision, or thinking about you in a way that is not honoring you, rather than being open to receiving their images, begin broadcasting your own pictures back to them. If you want them to see you as strong and powerful, send an image to them of yourself as strong and powerful. If you think of how you are wrong, you will send that image to them and they will find more ways to make you wrong.

*See everyone as
expanding and growing,
and you will see yourself
that way also.*

Begin broadcasting positive pictures to others. See them as achieving their goals and creating success. You can take responsibility for sending out high pictures of yourself and others. See the gems that lie buried in people. Acknowledge them when you see them, speak of their progress, their growth and beauty. If they want to give you a negative story of their life, do not sympathize but go into a role of compassion and help them see the gifts the situation is giving them. If you hear people speaking of negative things immediately send them positive pictures and change the conversation.

Hold an image of your higher purpose, then the thoughts and pictures that come into your mind will lead in that direction. You wonder if the pictures you get in your mind are the truth or just something you made up. When you receive or become aware of images about your path, you may wonder if it is what you are to do or if it is just wishful thinking or incorrect information.

If you ask for guidance,
trust the messages that come
into your mind.

Sometimes they may be simple, telling you the next step. It may be something as mundane as going to the post office or writing a letter. Some of you want to know your path for many months and years ahead and yet, if you knew it, it would only be a probable form, and one that could perhaps limit you. Some of you would become overwhelmed and find it hard to start. You might even find it less than joyful to know your whole future in advance. If you want more than you have right now, you can have it by trusting. Once you are determined to have abundance, what will come is even more than you could picture. If you want a vision of what to do with your life and you do not have it, it may simply be a matter of time. You may be getting prepared for that vision. You can bring anything you want to consciousness. If you feel blocked you can find answers by asking for them. You can evolve any situation with an image of light, and you can release any problem to the universe to resolve for you in the highest way.

Sometimes the greatest sense of joy can come from knowing you are not alone, that if you ask for guidance and assistance it will be there. If you are ready to link up with the universe you can have anything you want. You are not alone; if you are centered on your highest purpose you will find every door opening. The universe will give you ideas and assistance; people will reach out to you with help, money, advice, love, and support. Make the commitment. Do it now. Go for your highest purpose. Hold steady that vision of your highest good and be open for surprises.

All of you have pictures of what it would mean to love yourself more. For some of you it might mean a better job, or the resolution of a problem. If you want more self-love, the first challenge is to see if you can evolve your pictures of self-love. Everything you thought of as loving to yourself two years ago, you most probably have right now. Yet somehow when you got it you did not feel as loved as you expected. Look at what you want right now and ask, "What is the essence behind it?" If you want, for instance, a new place to live, what is the essence behind it? What do you really want? It may be peace and quiet, or more sunlight. You can get all of those things in different ways, right now.

Every time you think of the future you project energy into it, even if you mumble, "I never get things done," or "I don't know why this happened to me," or "I wish I hadn't done it." Every comment you make is directing energy, towards the past, the present or the future. If you could become aware of even one hundredth of the thoughts you are sending out into the future and evolve them, within a month you would know delight that exceeds all of your pictures today. Every single statement you make about yourself, to a friend or even to yourself becomes a truth. You project energy every moment. If you want a better future, speak of it, picture it, say it to others. Only you can create for yourself what you want. It is the greatest power, honor and gift you have ever been given.

PLAYSHEET

1 | Take a situation in your life you would like to understand; perhaps to learn why you created it or what it is teaching you. Write it here.

I would like to understand my insecurity, jealousy, anger, & fears.
I understand the nature of it & learning how to cope.
I know once I succeed I will graduate & that itself could limit me. I will succeed & live a happy abundant life.

2 | Sit quietly, relax, and close your eyes. Imagine you are holding the situation in your hands. Imagine light pouring into this situation, and release it to your higher self. See yourself receiving answers. Think of nothing else but this situation for five or ten minutes.

3 | In what way is this situation going to add to your personal power as you move through it? What is it teaching you? What soul qualities are you developing (such as love, patience, tolerance, and trust)? As you understand this situation, you will move through it more rapidly.

VII

Evolving Your
Inner Images:
Releasing the True Self

You carry many images of who you are that sit in a matrix of energy around your body. What are images? They are pictures of reality you hold in your mind. You use them as models to judge if you are good or bad, to decide how you will act and speak, and whom you will be with. They also create your boundaries and limits, and determine how far you can go. A lifetime is a journey out of darkness into light; through evolving your images you can bring more light into your life.

All of you have basic definitions you live by. You may see yourself as being strong, hard-working, intelligent, fun-loving, generous, kind, friendly. You create your experience of reality based on your image of yourself as a man or a woman. Your particular images determine your limits. If you see yourself as generous, for instance, you will either have to be generous all the time or judge yourself harshly when you are not generous.

Your definition of yourself as a man or a woman greatly influences your behavior.

Group images of women tend to involve serving, taking care of others, being responsible for relationships, being nice, being liked. Images of men focus on being assertive and strong, and ignoring feelings.

Many viewpoints of reality come from religious upbringing. For a moment, pause and look within. Go back to your childhood and ask what images you carry within you about the nature of the universe that come from your religious upbringing. You may think there is a God who punishes you when you are bad and rewards you when you are good. You may be afraid of the dark side of yourself. You might think you have no religion, yet everyone has a religious orientation, even if it is the belief in intuition and your creative self. Religious or philosophical beliefs are among the strongest images people have; they determine what you think about the nature of the universe and how you respond to it. Do you imagine you will be rewarded if you are good? Do you think that certain types of behavior are good and others are not? Those ideas often come from your religious background.

Your parents passed many of their images on to you. You selected your parents for the images they would give you that would bring to consciousness the inner and outer self you chose to work on in this lifetime. Think of your parents for a moment. Who are they? Think of some of their beliefs about money and abundance. Do you have feelings about those beliefs, either good or bad? Think about how your parents feel or felt about their relationship to each other. Take the parent that is the same sex as you. What does he or she believe about being a man or a woman? Do you share those images? Think about your parent of the opposite sex. What images does he or she have? Do you see yourself with any of those patterns in your relationships?

Imagine that you are standing in the center of a circle and around you are all the people you are close to. Each friend holds a vision of who you are. As you stand in this circle, allow yourself to bring to consciousness the images you are receiving from your friends. Pretend you are facing someone you are very close to—a husband, a wife, a friend, a loved one. Who is this person? What pictures is he or she sending to you about who you are? What images are you sending to this person? As you think of what you are sending, look at this person's soul right now and ask if there are images you could send that would help him or her evolve. You can help people grow by focusing on their potential. What pictures would you like this person to hold of you? See him or her sending you those images.

*Pay attention to the pictures
you send people. Are you
holding them back, or
helping them rise higher
with your images?*

People absolutely pick up the images you hold of them. Often, long-term relationships cannot survive because people are not willing to change their pictures of each other. One may hold on to an old image of the other as immature and irresponsible long after the other wants to change that behavior. Because of that image, it may be harder for the other to change. All of you have experienced yourself around your parents, who may hold onto very old images of you. Sometimes you go to them with your newfound strength, grown up and mature, and you find within five minutes you are acting out old, immature roles. Rather than feeling unhappy with yourself, use the opportunity to look at the images your parents hold of you, and realize how affected you can be by other people's views of who you are.

The minute you become aware of other people's pictures of you, telepathically send them a higher image. Often you accept their pictures without question, and not only accept them, but act them out. When you do so, you are living other people's scripts for you, rather than writing your own. You are dancing on their stage. As long as you do this, people who do not hold high thoughts about you will be detrimental to be around. But once you learn to recognize their images, you can begin to change them by sending them new pictures of yourself. Then you can be around them without being affected by their images—if you choose to be around them.

One way to free yourself from the grip of a rigid inner image is to exaggerate it in your mind. Say you are criticizing yourself for acting like a child around your parents, or falling into old behavior. Rather than resisting acting this way around your parents, exaggerate it in your mind. Really get into acting like a child. This enables you to see more clearly what those images are. As you exaggerate your images, you stop running from and fearing them, and they cease to control you. Often as you exaggerate behavior, it triggers your humorous side, which also frees you from the grip of that behavior.

You can change or eliminate those obsessive thoughts and pictures you flash over and over in your own mind. Sometimes they are pictures of pain, or memories of a time when someone abandoned or hurt you, or of a time when you did not get what you wanted. Many people experience a constant flow of negative pictures. Much of it comes from a cultural image of scarcity, that there is not enough, that you must work hard and struggle to get what you want, that someone else's success takes away from yours. That is an image I see people uniting to change. Pioneers of the New Age, those people who are learning about spiritual transformation, higher consciousness and love, are working to broadcast new, higher, lighter images to the world, including pictures of abundance.

Pictures are easier for people to pick up than words.

As a spiritual teacher, I am constantly broadcasting energy, transmitting images of love and peace through my thought-impulses. If you would like someone to change, send him or her images. For instance, say you want a person to be more productive. Rather than criticize (which sends a negative picture and reinforces the very behavior you would like to see changed), imagine the person being productive. Rather than point out the person's lack of accomplishments, acknowledge and praise each instance of the productivity you would like to see more of. You will be assisting him or her with your picture. And, whether or not the person changes, you will find the energy between you lighter.

Obsessive thoughts and feelings about a relationship, such as jealousy or pain, are keyed into your emotional aura, which is often very undeveloped compared to your mind. You are taught to value your mind and intellect more than your emotions, so there is much more attention paid to evolving the mind than the emotions. How free are you from the grip of your emotions? It is essential you become aware of the pictures you are carrying in your mind. When you find yourself flashing a negative picture over and over, it is simply a cry from your emotions for attention and help, and most of all, for love. For instance, if you are feeling exceptionally jealous, and you are constantly flashing pictures in your mind of your loved one seeing someone else, there is a part of you that is feeling rejected or abandoned by your own higher self.

Your soul is integrating all the parts of you and bringing them up to higher consciousness. Images that are obsessively painful are a cry from that part of you which most longs to be nurtured, to be loved and united with your higher self. If you catch that part showing you negative pictures, convert those pictures into symbols. If someone is pushing you away, see him symbolizing an energy within you. Imagine that he represents a part of you that is pushing your higher self away, and imagine yourself embracing and loving that part.

Everyone has a side that does not want to be light, joyful or high in its images or thoughts. Take that side and imagine you are exposing it to the sunlight, letting it breathe fresh air; visualize light coming into your dark or gloomy side. Within hours you will feel less negative. Every time you do not allow this side to take over, you strengthen your will and increase your connection to your higher self.

Beliefs such as "I am a good person, I am a spiritual person, I am a loving person" both determine your behavior and can limit you. If you define yourself with a fixed image, such as "I am a nice person," you will constantly be judging what you do as nice or not nice. If nice is defined rigidly for you, such as "nice people always say thank you," and someone you like doesn't say it, you will have to either change your definition of nice or judge your friend as not nice. An inflexible image will trap you in the world of polarities; right vs. wrong, good vs. bad. Expand your definitions of who you and other people are. Examine and unlock your images, let them become flexible and open rather than judgmental and closed. As long as you are comparing all your actions to fixed images of how you should be, you will be caught in the world of judgment and unable to evolve to higher levels.

To release images, become consciously aware of them. Honor your conscious mind. The time you spend analyzing yourself, from a peaceful state, brings your unconscious into consciousness; through this process evolution occurs. Every time you find a negative or limiting self-image, imagine light coming into it. You need not do anything else. (If you want to put more energy into it, you can find a symbol and play with it, healing the symbol.) Simply imagining light coming into the picture will change it. Use your imagination consciously.

What do you want? You may spend a great deal of time thinking of what you do not want, filling your mind and spirit with pictures of injuries or wrongs that were done to you. Every time you flash those pictures in your mind, you are literally sending them out to the future and creating them again. Negative things happen to you only to show you an image carrying that is not aligned with your higher good. Thank anything you respond negatively to, anything you see as a problem, for bringing your attention to a part of you that needs healing and more light.

Use *your imagination to picture*
the highest healing path you can take,
to create a vision of why you are here.

Ask yourself, "What is the most spiritual thing I can do
with my life?" Beyond the forms you create, what is your
highest aim? What is the most important thing you want to
do? It may be that you want to evolve your soul. You may
want to grow as fast as you can comfortably handle, or
broadcast healing. Hold that vision every day. Go as high
as you can with your imagination. Fantasize about your
perfect life. The higher you go, the more quickly the images and thoughtforms that do not fit your growth will
dissolve. Do not reach ahead just a year or two but ask,
"What could be my greatest accomplishment during this
lifetime?" Do not worry about the form or how you will
do it. Every time you create one picture or vision, you
open the door to an even greater picture. Hold an image in
front of you. Let the energy of that image come into your
body. Become consciously aware of the light in everything
you do, and you will evolve rapidly in this lifetime.

Know that other people will reflect back to you every
image you carry within. If they say something negative to
you, and evoke a strong response, thank them for reflecting back to you an image of yourself you need to change.

When you carry images such as "I am powerful, I truly
love and value myself, I have enough money, enough love,
etc." you will begin to see those images sent back to you.
Consciously send others higher images. Hold a vision of
your higher self in everything you do. Honor the higher
self in everyone you meet, and you will find it honored
in you.

PLAYSHEET

1 | Write out a description of yourself in as many words
as you like. For instance, "I am a spiritual person."

I am a very cute & attractive
gay boy who is in shape & fit.
I know my body & looks are
imp. & it shows.

I am also very kind, generous
considerate, honest, loving, & easy
to get along with. Integrity & dignity.

I am a "healer" & respect for
spiritual realm. I like to
meditate & work on healing &
working my spirit & soul.

I have a great life, a wonderful
career that I created & I
am Happy !!

2 | Now expand this description, make it an even higher picture of who you are. Speak of yourself in the most complimentary, glowing terms you can, being truthful, of course. For instance, "I am a hardworking, loving person who cares deeply for other people. I make my spiritual growth a priority. I practice, as often as I can, unconditional love." Make this description as high and loving as you can.

I deeply + unconditionally care for others releasing prejudice + w/ most right/wrong framework. I believe that all people are loving + kind & giving. I am able to be solid & secure w/ my emotions. I am able to trust & receive love in my relationship. I am patient + I practice active listening.

Face my fears w/ more calm & positive think

3 | Notice how you felt as you wrote the second description. The more you can see yourself from a higher view, the more accurately you are seeing who you are.

VIII

Finding Your
Deepest Truth

This lifetime is a journey of finding your deepest level of truth. Every situation in your life that is causing you struggle or pain is an area in which you are learning about being true to your soul.

You have many roles you play, and you experience different truths at different times. You may rehearse a speech, but when you go to see someone you find yourself saying something completely different. So you ask, "What is truth?" What is true one moment may not be true the next. Is truth fluid or is there a deeper truth that will last from moment to moment? All of you are fluid at the personality level, with many identities. Your soul, your core self, holds that deeper truth.

Compassion is the
ability to put yourself
in the other person's shoes.

Finding truth means coming from your heart and moving closer to your soul. Finding truth means holding every situation up to the light. What is that light? It comes foremost from the heart and is a deep level of compassion. In developing the quality of compassion you will be developing the ability to come from your deeper truth. All of you know people who cause you pain by not honoring or valuing you. You may want something from them that you are not getting. It can be on a business or a personal level. The situation can always be handled by coming from a deeper level of compassion.

You may say, "What is the benefit of coming from my deepest truth? I think I will just plow along and tackle things in my normal way." The benefit is the joy, the peace, and the serenity that so many of you desire.

Truth also comes from the feeling level. How many times have you had a feeling to call somebody and found that he was thinking of you when you did, and it was the perfect time to reach him? How many times have you had a feeling that it was not the time to call someone, but you ignored it and called anyway, and found the energy did not work between you, or she was not home? Every one of you has the ability to fine tune your sensing of energy and the sensing of the truth within you. How do you find this deeper inner truth? How do you step outside of all of the images you live by and the roles you play?

*You do not have to go through
pain and struggle to grow.*

The doorway to deeper truth is awareness. It is paying attention to, and holding up, the vision of truth. The more you act from integrity, the more evolved you become.

Every situation in your life that requires truth from you, that requires you to reach into a deeper level of your being, is an opportunity to grow. The more pain and struggle you experience, the greater the amount of energy you clean up when you come from your deeper level. Thank those situations in your life that seem difficult or painful. Know that they are opportunities to reach a deeper truth. Not a truth that will separate you, bring you anger, vengeance, or justification, or make the other person wrong and you right or vice versa, but a truth that will allow you to connect at a deeper level. To raise your energy higher, go inward and ask if you are withholding from yourself the truth of what you feel or think about the other person. If you do not let yourself see the truth, you will have another person and another sent your way until you do get in touch with your deepest truth.

For instance, you may have always wanted affection and nurturing from your partner. You get into relationships that don't satisfy these deeper needs, and you tell yourself you shouldn't and don't need it. Your deepest truth is that you do need it, and until you get in touch with that truth and act upon it you will continually experience pain.

Every time you act and speak from truth and integrity you lighten your energy. Your aura is like a fog. Each time you speak the truth the energy around you becomes finer and lighter, until the sunlight is pouring through it into your body. Every drama in your outer life is a reflection of a drama in your inner life. Every person you are interacting with in your outer life symbolizes an interaction of energy that is going on within you. Think of a person in your life you are struggling with. Imagine you are looking at yourself through his or her eyes. Put yourself in his or her place. Go into your heart and see yourself coming from a deep, compassionate level of truth with that person. See the person responding with joy as the energy between you grows lighter. If you have been feeling angry or resentful of someone, and you come from your deepest truth, you may realize that you have felt competitive with him or her, or that you really love the person even if he or she disappointed you. From that place you can let go of the hurt and speak to this person with love.

Every person and event offers you an opportunity to clean up your energy, evolve yourself, and move higher. The greatest reward is that once an issue is cleared up you will never have to deal with it again. You cannot be hurt by another person unless you are hurting yourself. You cannot be betrayed, undervalued or unloved unless you are doing it to yourself by not valuing and loving yourself.

*You have the greatest power of all,
the ability to heal yourself.*

When you heal yourself, everything around you that represented your inner struggle dissolves. You can heal yourself by speaking the truth from a deep level of compassion. For instance, you may be thinking that someone doesn't value your feelings. As you look one level deeper at the truth, you say to yourself, "She is just being herself and she isn't very aware of anyone's feelings, not just mine." Or, "She's in pain herself and doesn't realize she's hurting me." As you look even deeper, you see that you have let her treat you that way, that you haven't valued your own feelings either, and that there have been many times you wanted to speak up. You can continue to look deeper, until you feel a release from the pain, and acceptance for the other person.

Look at the different personalities within you. One is very strong, another observes everything you do with detachment, another is young and emotional, and another is very wise. If there is any drama going on around you, you can be assured that there is a drama going on inside of you between your various parts.

One woman felt betrayed by her girlfriend when a secret she had confided was spoken to another. Upon closer examination, she realized that she had betrayed her true self in many ways, and that the outer drama was to show her what she was doing to herself.

Coming from compassion means coming from truth. How often do you rehearse in your mind what you are going to say to someone because you are justifying yourself, coming from ego, talking about how great you are, or how right you are? Every time you find yourself mentally rehearsing a situation (as all of you do, over and over) ask, "Can I come from one deeper level of truth?" You can always find one way in which to be more loving, understanding and compassionate.

Finding your deepest truth means looking within. It means not blaming other people, not playing the victim and not spending time feeling sorry for yourself. When you look more deeply at any situation, you can always see that you set it up for your growth. In any situation you feel you were a victim you always had an inkling of what was going on, and ignored opportunities to change things.

As you look more deeply at things that really bother you, I want to propose a thought: Nothing you are upset about is caused by what you think. For instance, you may be upset that your friend accused you of doing something you didn't do. Upon deeper examination, you will find that it is a recreation of an earlier pain, played out over and over in changing scenery with different people until you resolve it. It may be a reenactment of a childhood drama in which you were accused of things you didn't do. Pain, anger, or resentment you feel now almost always comes from a similar childhood experience. You recreate the pain so that you can move beyond it. Next time you feel angry at someone, stop. Close your eyes and go within. See that you have had similar experiences before. Realize that you are reliving some childhood decision and that now is an opportunity to end this pattern in your life and come from your deepest truth. Realize other people are only drawn to play out certain roles with you to help you evolve. Let go of any anger or blame you have towards them.

You have the ability to know your truth.

The truth is that you are a great being; you have within you the compassion, courage, strength, and wisdom to come from a high level at all times. You act out roles that do not reflect the greatness of who you are, but they are only roles and not your true self.

The more you can be aware of the thoughts coming into your mind, the more control you will have over the drama that is happening inside of you. You can think of your thoughts as little men that come marching up, one, two, three. If you could stop each one and hold it up to the light you would find better ways of thinking. It is a matter of attention and awareness, taking each thought you have and examining it to see if it is really a true statement or not.

Coming from the truth means paying attention to energy. Often you do not notice what is happening until the situation is so painful you must go inward, meditate, think, and put yourself in another person's shoes. That may be the whole reason you created the situation. If you were to do these things frequently, life would be easier. If, when you felt uncomfortable, you went inward and opened your heart with compassion, things would not reach crisis level.

Every time you rehearse in your mind what you will say to people, you are sending energy into your future interaction with them. Often you rehearse so that you may come from a deeper and more compassionate level in your actual communication. If you can make this the goal of mental rehearsal you will find your relationships clearing up. If you are rehearsing to protect or justify yourself or get something from another person, you will find yourself uncomfortable when you are speaking to him or her. You will have an incomplete communication, one which will lead to further energy expenditure and perhaps further struggle. That is why it is better to wait, when you are angry with someone, until you can come from a loving space of your deepest truth, rather than act out of anger.

Why is it so difficult to look another person in the eyes and come from your deepest truth? Is it because of fear of loss? Is it a fear you won't be loved if you reveal your deeper being? For some of you, it is a fear of being vulnerable. It is often easier to play out roles that say, "I am strong and invincible, I am a perfect person," than to take down the walls and uncover who you are to another person. When you have nothing to lose, it certainly is easier to come from your deepest truth. The universe may put you in a situation in which you have nothing to lose so that you can experience coming from your deepest truth and thus clean up a relationship. But you do not need to get to the point where you have nothing to lose to speak the truth.

Imagine in front of you, right now, anyone with whom you would like to clean up an issue or make the relationship between you better. See the person's face in front of you, his or her eyes looking at you with complete understanding and compassion. Picture the person accepting your truth. Mentally say something to him or her that will take both of you higher.

*As you think over
what you will say to someone,
hold the image of your deepest truth,
and practice loving ways of expressing it.*

Each time you rehearse, you become more efficient and confident, and you will find an even better way to express yourself. Be kind and gentle with yourself. When you first begin to speak truth, you may find there is a part of you that criticizes you for not having done it better. If you find yourself reviewing past events, don't make yourself wrong for the way you spoke or acted. Instead, see that you did the best you knew how. You can send energy backward or forward, so the energy you send from your heart can heal a situation in the past. Recognize that what you learned opened up your truth.

At a certain level, everyone knows the truth about each other. You may try not to see the truth, but you do indeed know it at some level. There is no hiding from each other, and there is no need to do so. You are a magnificent, beautiful, alive human being, doing the very best you know how. All of you are deeply aware of each other, and when you match your words and actions precisely to that awareness, you evolve. You may think it is not kind to speak your mind, to speak up, if you hold an image that it is not understanding and sympathetic. You may think you are doing someone a favor by covering up your feelings, but you may be setting up a drama where the only way out is through the truth. You may even have to end a relationship if that is what it takes to detach enough to speak the truth.

Honoring your deepest truth is a great gift to you and to the other person.

This does not mean that truth should be expressed by making the other person wrong. Your deepest truth will be spoken with love for yourself and for the other person. If what you say is damaging or harmful to the other person, then you have not come from your deepest truth which is always loving.

For instance, a woman was dating a man who later left her for another woman. She was very hurt, and on the surface wanted to strike out at him and make him feel less about himself. Her first inclination, feeling hurt and rejected, was to make him wrong. As she got in touch with her deeper truth, she realized that she truly loved him, wanted him to be a friend, and saw that what she did in the past—close her heart and walk away—was not her truth. Even though she felt hurt, she was able to recognize the love underlying the pain and express that love in her communication. Within several months, the man came back to her, a new level of respect and love for her in his heart.

Many of you hold up an image of truth, and yet you deceive yourself about who you are. You do so when you imagine yourself as a victim, for you are not a victim; you are a high, powerful being. You deceive yourself any time you do not acknowledge your beauty, wisdom and power. Any time you find yourself sinking into feelings of self-pity or depression you are deluding yourself and not coming from your truth. When you deceive yourself, you carry that energy within you, and you will see it played out in the world around you. If you are telling yourself that you are not powerful, you begin to set up a resonance in your energy field and you attract people and events to you that mirror that thought. As you clean up your energy, become truthful about who you are, so will the universe reflect that truth.

Take a situation you want to improve with someone and imagine that the very wisest part of you—your highest being, the confident, powerful, loving part of you—is handling it. See a smile on the other person's face, and talk to the person in your mind. Any time you find yourself speaking in a way that is not confident and high, first acknowledge that you are doing the best you know how. Appreciate all the parts of you. It is not going to heal you to make the high part right and the emotional part wrong. Keep focusing on the higher part of your self and give the insecure part love, and it will evolve.

Watch as you rehearse scenes in your mind. Observe yourself playing out your roles; look at the reaction you anticipate from the other person. Notice that what you expect you often get. Hold in your mind a vision of yourself releasing and speaking your truth, in a most loving and compassionate way, putting yourself in the other person's shoes. See it as the highest and most healing thing you can do for the relationship. Imagine the other person responding with warm understanding. A sense of joy and energy will surely follow, for it takes far more energy to withhold the truth, deny and not see it, than to see it, speak and act upon it.

Initially it may take energy to open up, but consider the overall results: the amount of time you spend thinking about the situation and the pain you feel will be over. You will have hours of free time. What will you do with all that extra time?

You release creative energy when you free yourself from any deceptive situation. As you speak, practice accuracy and precision with your words. Watch with care every statement you make and attitude you assume, so as to negate any tendency to emotional misrepresentation. Don't overemphasize details or exaggerate the usual and commonplace into the unusual and uncommon. Develop the ability to produce a true picture of things as they really are and it will help you create what you want in physical reality. As you match your words with the truth, your energy will go higher and higher. You will have more physical energy, more peace and better connections with people. Those friends who do not want to come from a deeper truth with you will be replaced by new people who do. The old, uncomfortable situations you have set up will not be able to survive in your new level of light, and they will dissolve.

PLAYSHEET

1 | Is there anyone in your life you have withheld truth from? Write down what you really want to say to him or her. Let it come out without judgment.

2 | Now that you have written it, is there an even deeper level of truth you can come from, one that is softer, more compassionate and acknowledging of the other person as a loving individual? Rewrite what you wrote above.

3 | You can keep doing this until you see the real issue be-
tween you. Then imagine light and joy between you as
you release the truth.

IX

Journey into Light: Going Higher

There are many levels of energy in the universe, from the coarser or denser levels all the way up to the levels of great masters. The coarser levels exist as heavy emotions and negative thoughts. The higher levels are beyond polarities, beyond good and bad, beyond the storms of the emotions. They are levels of increasing love, light and personal power. There are lessons at every level, and one of the easiest ways to go higher is to acknowledge the lessons as challenges and opportunities for growth. As you go higher the challenges do not stop, but they do change in their nature. You could not grow without challenges. Your attitude towards them either helps you go higher and grow faster, or keeps you in the dense levels longer.

The more you dislike problems, the more you rebel against things not going your way, the longer your problems will stay with you. These denser levels of energy are like quicksand, pulling you down. When you are caught in them your thoughts revolve around what you consider to be problems. As you move to higher levels, your thoughts move also, and you begin thinking about what your soul can accomplish, how your soul can evolve your personality, and how you can follow your spiritual path. Each of you in your own way seeks to know yourself. To sense energy, you must know the self; put energy and time into the self, and become aware of who you are and what you are thinking. You can increase self-awareness by paying attention to your thoughts. Record them and divide them into categories. In each category, such as thoughts about an intimate relationship, see how high your level of thinking is. Thoughts that are negative or self-destructive are on the dense or lower side; thoughts that are positive, optimistic or healing are on the finer, higher side.

One way out from denser energy levels into higher energy is through your will and intent. You can go higher by simply affirming that you intend to go higher. Battling with the problems or struggling with the issues gets you bogged down. Sometimes the mind loves to get involved in arguing, in resisting and struggling, which keeps you in the lower energies.

Every time you come to an issue that you cannot resolve, affirm to yourself that you have the will and intent to go higher. The imagination has the ability to take you higher by creating a vision of what you want to be.

The ability to make yourself right rather than wrong will help you grow faster.

Learn to affirm that everything you do, whether you understand why or not, is perfect for your growth. Many of you have chosen a fast course of evolution, wanting to evolve quickly all at once. Many of you want to complete many parts of your soul's journey during this life, choosing a steep path of growth rather than a slow and gradual one.

Transformation of the planet begins in transformation of the self. Evolution starts with the commitment and intent to go higher. Pay attention to your thoughts and your emotions, and become aware of the messages in the challenges you are going through. Avoid getting stuck in issues; look at them as if they were to your side rather than in front of you. Focus on what you want rather than what you don't want. Once you have demonstrated to the universe that you intend to go higher, you will be flooded with new insights on what to do. The universe will begin to show you the way.

Many of you feel that your struggles are insurmountable. Some of you struggle to establish a deep love or the right connection with another. Some of you wrestle with your appearance, diet, nutrition, or exercise. You may debate—is this the right way or is that the right way? All of you have the inner knowledge to know what is the right way for you. You have the wisdom if you listen to your inner self. You have an abundance of information coming to you right now. Perhaps one of the greatest challenges facing all of you is knowing what information to use and what information not to use. Information is flooding the planet. There are books to read, advice on what to eat, what not to eat, how to feel, how not to feel. I see a great deal of confusion at all these facts. Some of you feel that if you could force yourself to eat all the right foods, follow all the rules and work on yourself constantly you would be a perfect, evolved person. The ego and the mind would like evolution to be structured and formulated; not so the soul.

Childhood programming and a desire to be part of the group teach you that what everyone else is doing is the right way. But each of you is completely different. Your nutritional needs, exercise and sunlight requirements, relationships, desires, and work are different.

*There is no one right way
to evolve or pursue your soul's path.
It is up to you to choose
whatever is best for you.*

Awareness of your own energy will tell you what is good for you. When you see all the books you have in your home, hear about all those weight loss processes, for instance, don't ask yourself, "What *should* I try?" but ask instead "What would I *love* to do?" The things that you would love to do, books that you would delight in reading, things you can't wait to try are good for you. Those that you feel you should or must do are not appropriate for who you are. You can use your will power, as you call it, to make yourself, force yourself to follow other people's programs, but always your inner being will undo what you do. Then you will label yourself a failure, or feel you have no will power. It is not will power as you know it that will evolve you, but the intent to go higher, and letting the changes come naturally. Allow your feelings to flow moment to moment, act upon them, and know them. For instance, with food, simply become quiet and relaxed, and ask yourself what you crave and what sounds delicious. Even if you desire chocolate or something you have labeled as bad for you, it may be that your physical body needs some substance in chocolate to maintain its vibration and resonance, and the only way it knows how to get it is through chocolate. You may need only a little, and once you take away all the shoulds and shouldn'ts, you will find your body naturally craving other things that are better for it.

When you speak of books, all the books you *should* read and the knowledge you *should* have, be aware that sometimes it is only one paragraph or one page of a book you need to read to get what you want. We are speaking of the quality of discrimination, knowing the difference between what is good for you and what is not.

Each of you has a personal map of reality, your own assumptions, a unique philosophy about life and a personal belief system. One of the challenges I will offer you is to look at your map. What is a personal map? For one person a map may say, "There is not enough love in the universe." For another, their map may say, "Every time I open up to another person I get hurt." Your maps are based on your childhood and lifetime experiences. They are based on your experience of how your energy has flowed out and how you have been received by others, especially those you loved or wanted love from.

If any area of your life is not working, one of your beliefs in that area needs to be changed.

It is time to either get a new map or revise the one you have. You cannot change it by forcing yourself, however. You can change it by calmly and firmly telling yourself that you intend to go higher, and that you do not plan to get caught up in the argument or in the issues. It may sound simple, but this is all you need to do to start movement out of the conflict. Once you affirm that you intend to go higher, the universe will begin to show you the answers.

Another way to move out of denser, negative energy is to be aware of the telepathic messages and emotions you send out, for they have the power to affect many people. Whatever you send out is what you draw back in. Take responsibility for the thoughts and emotions you send out, for they go out into the universe and create the events and circumstances that come back to you.

You can learn how to send positive thoughts and emotions to other people, or project them out into your own future where you can meet up with them. Every thought you send out is magnetic because it creates and brings to you events, people, and things. It does so by resonating with those things you think of and thus it determines what is drawn to you.

You can assist mankind
in achieving peace
by evolving your thoughts.

Every thought you send out creates events in the universe, attracts people to you. Even more than that, every thought you send out is creating the transformation of the planet. You may not feel that one person can have that much effect on the overall energy of the planet, and yet one high, healing thought can cancel out 10,000 or more negative ones. The higher the healing thought, the more lower ones that get cancelled. It is not just yourself you are helping when you evolve your thoughts, but everyone around you. You do not even have to know them personally or be physically around them. Healing, positive thoughts go out into your neighborhood and your community and help everyone who is reaching upward.

Imagine you are sitting up above the earth, as you have seen it from the satellite photos, and imagine that a great deal of mankind below you is thinking about mundane things, or is lost in lower thoughts. Imagine that the higher you go, the more people you can reach with your finer and higher thoughts. People going about their daily lives, looking for answers to their problems, can use the healing broadcast you are sending out. Mankind is going through a transformation. You are at a crossroads; in one direction lies peace and abundance, in the other, conflict and scarcity. It is time to become aware of your own personal thoughts on an ongoing, daily basis. Every time you hate something, every time you feel angry at yourself, every time you put yourself down or make yourself wrong you are contributing to the planetary choice of scarcity. Every time you allow yourself to have more, allow yourself to feel good, or love something, you are contributing to the planetary path of abundance.

PLAYSHEET

1 | List the main things you think about (career, friends,
family, money, car, clothes, food, health, etc.). Rate
how positively you feel about each of these things on a
scale of 1 to 10—1 being negative, 10 being positive.

1. my biz = 10
2. my honey = Derrick = 8
3. humming birds = 10
4. having a Dog = 8
5. House = 8
6. Tennis = 10
7. Massage + taking care of myself = 10
8. vacation = 10
9. Mental landscape = 7
10. Love = 10
11. Peace = 10
12. Plan = 5
13. issues = 8
14. state of the world = 6
15. Body = 10

Past pain + memories = 3

2 | How high and positive do your thoughts look?

pretty high. I do think
about bad memories, hurt.
+ violence + loss. - there
are my negative thoughts
during the day that I
have been working hard
to stop + be more positive

3 | Take one area that you rated as low, and write down a positive picture you could hold about that area.

- Past pain & memories that make me fearful & irresponsible of recieving love & uncomfortable to be present in my mind & body. (including thoughts of violence, death, & unable to ~~how~~ hold good thoughts due to being afraid of bad violent thoughts)

(✳) my positive picture d see is being able to control my reaction towards bad thoughts. d envision myself being unbothered by unwanted emotions & thoughts. d see my mental fortress becoming beautiful, clear & graceful. d envision myself holding positive thoughts for longer periods. d envision myself mastering my core issues. d envision myself full of joy, love, & abundance.

X

Learning
Unconditional Love

Unconditional love means keeping your heart open all the time. To do so, you may need to let go of the expectations you have of other people, of wanting them to be anything other than what they are. It means letting go of any need for people to give you things, act in certain ways, or respond with love. Many of you wait for other people to be warm and loving before you are.

Unconditional love is learning
to be the source of love
rather than waiting for others
to be the source.

Unconditional love allows you to join with others and keep your personal boundaries intact. To be able to join with others, know your own boundaries. People desire to join with others, to have intimate connections, and yet at the same time to be separate. If you are fee ing suffocated in a relationship, being asked to do things you do not want to do, it is because you are not clear about your own boundaries Although it is easier to blame the other person, it is you who needs to get clear about your boundaries. On the other hand, if there are things you want from another person that you are not getting, it is because you are trying to use the other person to fill a space within you that only you can fill.

Take the example of a woman who feels suffocated in a relationship. She feels the man she is with s constantly asking for more than she wants to give—more time, attention, and commitment to the relationship. She blames him for being so demanding. However, the pattern lies within her and until she recognizes it she will continue to attract similar relationships. Often a pattern shows up as its opposite. She may attract either men who are demanding too much or men are unavailable and don't want an involvement.

This is a woman who has not come to terms with her sense of self. So long as she is not certain where she ends and other people begin, she will constantly be struggling to define her boundaries. She will shy away from commitments, because she experiences them as a loss of self-identity. Not being clear about who she is, she will feel pressured by demands or even simple requests. If she had clear boundaries, she would find it easy to say no. If she had clear boundaries she wouldn't attract relationships that keep testing her boundaries. Once she gets clear on how much of herself she wants to give, and on what the balance between herself and others feels right, she will attract relationships that fit that new picture.

Unconditional love transforms fear.

Fear is like a background noise that circles the planet, affecting many actions and decisions. It takes strength and courage to face what you fear. As you become aware of energy, you will also become aware of fear. The first place to examine it is in yourself, although it may be far more visible to you in other people. If, when you look at a friend or loved one, you can see clearly where he or she is closed or fearful, see if it is a reflection of a place within you that needs more love.

It is easier to see things in other people than in yourself. That is why the universe will often teach you something about yourself by putting you around people who show you what you are learning. You would not focus on that trait or part of them if you were not working on those issues yourself.

Fear can come from your thinking patterns. I see common thoughts that tell you you are bad and that if you do not watch out, you may be harmed. These are mass thoughts shared by many. You will at some point face them directly in yourself as you begin going upward into the higher levels of the universe. Fear shows up in thoughts that are very self-critical—wondering if you have disappointed someone, thinking that you aren't trying hard enough, or that you yourself are not enough.

If you discover your fears as you open to a new relationship, do not make yourself wrong. Fear is an undercurrent and the more you can discover it and face it the more you can heal it through your unconditional love and acceptance of yourself.

How do you discover fear? Look at some area of your life where you have a decision to make. Ask yourself if there are any reasons you do not feel free to make a decision to do what you want to do. Perhaps there is a fear that there will not be enough money, a fear that you cannot make it on your own, that you will not succeed, or a fear that others do not love you and will not want you if you do not live up to their expectations, or if you stand up for yourself. As you look at this decision, ask yourself, what would you do if you knew you were totally safe and protected, guided and loved by the higher forces of the universe? If you knew your soul was assisting you in every way possible, and if you knew you could fully trust your wiser self, would you make a different decision? This is one way of uncovering fear.

Fear is a place that has not yet discovered love.

Fear is often disguised as logical and rational reasons why something cannot be done. Sometimes it comes disguised as a feeling that other people are stopping you. There are many ways to disguise fear—blame it on others, refuse to take responsibility, decide you can't do it anyway so why try, get angry and quit, and many others. What ways do you use to cover up fear?

If you discover you are doing these things, the first step is to recognize that the reason you are avoiding something or feeling bad about another and yourself is because of fear, and that it is a place that requires your unconditional love. Love this part of you; do not make it wrong. Be willing to look directly at what you are avoiding. You don't have to apologize, cover up by acting strong, or think that you are a bad person. Once you recognize fear, it becomes much easier to deal with. It is only when it is in disguise that it can create separateness and pain.

One way to discover fear is to take something that you want to create, but fear you cannot, and list all the reasons why you cannot create it. Then, turn those reasons into positive statements of why you *can* create what you want. You will find that fear dissolves in the light of consciousness. Love is like the warm sun that shines on the ice; it melts and dissolves any barriers, any areas of pain. Like the ice, your fears will turn to water and evaporate.

When you notice yourself responding to other people with fear rather than love, perhaps pulling away from them, afraid that they will reject you, make you wrong, or ask too much of you, thank yourself for becoming aware of fear. Love that part of you that is afraid, and then begin to radiate unconditional love.

When you are judgmental or critical, you are most affected by other people's energy. If you look at people and think, "They ought to work harder, get their act together," these thoughts pull their negative energy into you. What you see in them is what you begin to experience in them, for as you focus on something you draw it out. What you fear you draw to you. Get in touch with that gentle loving part of you, your higher and wiser self, that guides you into being more loving.

When you experience uncomfortable barriers and boundaries between yourself and others, it is a sign that you need to transmit more love to others and to yourself. You may not choose to live with them, be close to them or around them all the time, but they will still benefit from your broadcast of love. Some of you try to put on a brave and strong front, acting in a way that says, "I will not be vulnerable or hurt." Yet, that very act creates fear and pain, attracting even more negative action from people that then requires an even braver exterior.

Look at the times you want to close your heart, the times at which you say, "I have had enough, this person is not being loving enough for me, I think I am going to leave." In every relationship, no matter how long-term or solid, there will always be a challenge to keep your heart open. How else do you learn unconditional love but by coming up against all those areas in which your heart is closed? Each time you come to a place in which you want to close your heart, you now have the opportunity to establish a new pattern, and keep it open. You may still choose to leave or change the nature of the relationship, but you can do so with love. You may think that the best friends are those who never challenge you, who never make you want to close your heart, and yet if you are with people who never challenge you to remain open and loving, you are not truly connecting with them in your heart. The heart always deals with issues of trusting, opening and reaching new levels of acceptance and understanding of others.

You learn to love by putting yourself in situations that challenge you to be loving.

Tolerance is an attribute of unconditional love. Smiling inwardly when people do things that used to upset you, sending them a warm blessing or thought of love, frees you from being affected by their behavior. The quality of tolerance is the ability to stay calm and unruffled no matter what happens, to allow people to be themselves and make their own mistakes. It allows you to provide that warm, safe harbor for them where they can bask in the steadfast light of your acceptance.

Whatever you give others is also a gift to yourself.

The ability to accept other people for who they are is a great challenge, and as you master it, so do you give that gift to yourself. If someone is yelling at you or talking in a tone of voice or a way that sparks anger, defensiveness, or sadness in you, begin sending him love telepathically. Bring yourself to a peaceful center and relax your breathing. As you send him love, do not expect him to quit yelling or respond in any way. Know as you send this love you are raising *your* vibration. Soon, either he will change or you will find that you are no longer creating situations where others are angry at you.

Relationships challenge you to keep your heart open and feel loving towards others. The quality of defenselessness is important. It is that feeling that you have nothing to defend, hide or apologize for. It comes from a feeling of self-acceptance, not justifying behavior that you want to improve, but knowing that making yourself wrong for it will only lock you into that behavior longer. People are often afraid to admit that they may be wrong, in pain or hurt. Sometimes, for instance, when you are feeling un-settled and out of your calm, clear center, you may try to put on a front, acting as if nothing is wrong. If instead, when you are with another, you allow yourself to express your true feelings, you open up a channel of communica-tion that can deepen your connection.

You may want everybody to think you are a perfect per-son, so you act out a role that says, "I'm fine, do not worry about me, I am tough and I don't need any help." That creates separateness between yourself and others and keeps you from love at the very time you most need it. Have you noticed how much love you feel towards others when they are vulnerable and admit that they are not sure how to handle something, rather than acting as if they know it all? Do not be afraid to be seen for who you are.

*If you have nothing to defend,
life becomes easier, for you do not
have to pretend to be anything you are not.*

Life is harder when you think you have to defend your beliefs, thoughts or self. I will suggest that most of the things you think you have to defend are beliefs and ideas that are not yours anyway. You rarely get offended and hurt when someone disagrees with the things you are sure about. The areas where you are not certain, where you feel insecure are those you often feel the most need to defend.

The next time you feel you have to defend something about yourself, ask yourself, why am I feeling I must defend this? Be willing to let your heart and wisdom smile upon people, sending them your love and acceptance. Do not feel you must say anything. Be who you are. If you do not know the answer to something, simply say, "I do not know." Do not try to be perfect all the time. Do not think that to be loved you must have all the answers, that you must never be afraid or look weak, for those of you who are willing to be vulnerable will find more love coming to you.

Forgiveness is part of unconditional love. Forgive yourself throughout the day for all the moments when you are not high, not loving and not wise. Forgive others for all the moments they are not high, loving and wise. As you forgive, you make it easier to become those things you want to be, and you make it easier for others to become them also.

People who respond to you in a way that seems to deny that you are a loving being are coming from a place of fear within themselves. If they ignore you, make you wrong, say unkind things, or act in a way that implies you are not their equal, realize that they are coming from fear. You do not need to respond to the fear within them by creating it within yourself. Instead, you can become a source of healing to those around you.

You attract situations into your life to learn from them. One way out and up is by responding with love. As you do so, every situation will change in its nature and character. By practicing, you can learn to broadcast love for longer and longer periods of time. Practice everywhere you go. Send love to the earth. Send love to everyone you meet. See if you can notice something beautiful about them.

*Love brings beauty
to everything and everyone.
Most of all, love brings beauty to you.*

When people are in pain, it is a powerful time to help them change their lives. Often when they are afraid, they are also ready to listen. If you perceive that people are afraid, that they do not feel loving towards themselves, it may be time to reach out, send them your unconditional acceptance and embrace them in your light.

Those who appear to have no fear, seeming to be the bravest, may need even more love than people who are willing to be vulnerable. Those who create pain in others, who are aggressive, bully people and make life miserable for those around them are usually the most in need of love. Send love to those who seem to have everything and those who seem to have power over you, such as your landlord, boss or parents. They only have power over you to the degree you let them; only your fear can create a sense of inferiority in you. If in any way you fear people in a position of authority or power over you, send them love. It will help stop any power struggles and attune you to a higher part of their being, where miracles and love are available.

As you become filled with light,
your power to affect the
world around you increases.

If people in your life are sending out negative energy and not meeting your expectations, it is important to send them unconditional love. They are simply being themselves, doing the best they know how. You will find great inner peace when you do not need others to act in a certain way to be happy yourself. You will become a radiating beacon of energy and the higher you go the further you can reach with your thoughts. When you send someone unconditional love, it is no longer possible for you to be harmed by his or her negative energy. If there is any situation in your life where you are feeling hurt, afraid or separated from others, begin sending them love and acceptance for who they are. This will heal you and them.

The more people act mean, the more they are afraid, and thus the more they need your love. Indeed those who are humble, vulnerable and defenseless most often have at their disposal an abundance of love. Send it to them also, but do not forget to send your love to those who appear to be the most unlovable, for they are the ones who are crying out the most loudly for love. Find reasons to love the unlovable, to care for people who act in destructive ways. There is not one person alive who does not grow from the broadcast of love. Whenever you give love it comes right back to you, changes your vibration and aura, and you become even more magnetic to love coming to you. It may not come from those you are sending love to, but it will come.

When you are feeling afraid for any reason, it is a time to connect with your higher self. When you felt afraid as a child, there was always someone or something that reassured you and took away the fear—a parent, relative or favorite stuffed animal. It was usually something outside of yourself, however. Part of your journey into light is to be able to create inside of yourself that sense of safety, that assurance that the world is friendly and that you are loved and protected by a caring and generous universe. Ask your soul to assist you. Calm your breathing and go inward until you find that place of trust.

When you are afraid, imagine that you are being held and embraced by the most loving friend you have ever had, one who cares for you unconditionally, who loves you whether you have high thoughts or low, who is by your side all the time, and embraces you with constant light. This is your soul. Know that you do have this friend you can call upon when you are afraid, who will help you connect with that higher part of yourself. You can also call upon the guides and masters, for whoever calls is always heard and sent love and guidance. All you need do is ask for the help or connection, and it will be there.

Even when things seem uncomfortable and dark, do not think you are off your path, for you are always reaching upward. Sometimes it may seem difficult and the path may feel steep. Other times you will find places where you are running, dancing and traveling with ease. Suspend judgment and make each stage of your growth easier by accepting what comes. Allow yourself to love the bumpy road as well as the smooth, and constantly thank yourself for your courage in reaching upward, in trying to go for the best and the highest that you know. Remember that you are a loving being, that you deserve love, and that you are, in essence, love itself.

PLAYSHEET

1 | Think of an area in your life you would like to change. Record here what changes you would make. (For example, I would buy, instead of rent, a place to live.)

2 | List below all the reasons you can't possibly create that change. These represent your unconscious fears. (For example, I can't possibly buy a house because I can't afford the monthly payments, I don't have enough for a down-payment.)

3 | Sit quietly and forgive every part of you that doesn't think you can create this change. Send all these doubtful, fearful voices love and acceptance.

4 | Turn these doubts into positive affirmations and begin saying them to yourself. You might want to put them on a poster where you will see them every day for a few weeks. (For instance, I can now afford the monthly payments, I receive the down-payment or its equivalent easily.)

XI

Handling Pain by Choosing to Grow

As you move to the higher levels of awareness, you may be faced with handling the energy of anger and pain within others and in yourself. Learning how to stay balanced and in your heart around those energies is part of the process of the soul's evolution toward light.

When you feel hurt and separated from another person, thinking he or she caused you pain or unhappiness, it may be time to examine what lessons you have chosen to learn by creating the situation. When you love people, there are times you feel pain and distance from them. If this happens, do not look for intellectual reasons. Do not try to discover who has hurt whom and who is to blame and who is in the right. It rarely does any good to argue back and forth, figuring out who is the good guy and who is the bad guy. This puts you into a power struggle with each other and takes you out of your heart connection.

Both people usually feel they are right and that the other person is unjustified in his or her approach. People usually feel that their own anger is justified, and that the other person's is not. When people feel hurt, most lash out at the other person as the cause of their pain. However, there is always pain inside before another can trigger it; the other person only acts as a catalyst to bring it out. The other person is *not* the cause. The cause is a pain within you. It is not an accident that the other person triggered it, either, for most often you choose loved ones and friends who push your buttons, so that you may learn and grow.

When you find yourself feeling hurt and yet righteously indignant, sure that you are the injured party and that someone owes you an apology, get silent for a moment before you lash out in anger. It is very easy to feel righteous, and yet righteousness separates you from those you want to love and feel close to. As the soul reaches for more light, one of its lessons is to learn not to make things right or wrong, but to stay in the heart with compassion. This involves being willing to see the other person's viewpoint and not feel you have to prove anything.

It is important to learn how to handle pain, for in doing so you allow your soul to become the captain of the ship. What is pain? Pain is an area in which the soul has not yet brought through sufficient light to allow the compassionate and gentle heart to shine forth. Pain is an area that is waiting for love.

When you are in pain, besides a natural tendency to blame another, there is a tendency to want to retreat, to withdraw and to close your heart. If you feel you are not being treated in a way you would like by a friend or a loved one, and that is causing you pain, it is better not to start by making him wrong and seeking an apology. Instead, start by looking within. Another person can only trigger pain when there is already pain within. He can only cause you to close your heart where your heart is already wanting to close. If there is no pain within, another cannot bring it out. You would only feel compassionate and sorry for him, not angry and threatened.

Pain is only triggered by another person when there is already pain within you.

Every time another person creates pain in you it is a gift. It is showing you an area in which your heart has not yet learned to be open. It is showing you a place where you may bring more light into yourself. You have drawn certain people into your life to show you the places where you need to become more open. Part of your lesson will be to stay open and loving even when they are acting in a way that used to cause you pain.

Before you approach the other person with recrimination, closing your heart and pulling away, creating more separateness and pain, stop. Ask yourself if you are willing to bring in light.

How does one bring in light when there is pain? First of all, it is important that you get away from the physical presence of the person who is causing you pain, while you begin to strengthen and draw light into yourself. Being physically near the other person (until you are quite a master at controlling energy) puts you into his aura. If the other person is in pain or is creating pain for you, being around him will make it harder to restore your own balance. If you find yourself in the midst of an argument, if you find yourself feeling hurt, wanting to strike out or withdraw, first, no matter what, physically distance yourself from him or her. Keep your silence until you have had an opportunity to be alone. Ask for a few moments to sit and think. Say that you do not want to speak in anger. Often it helps diffuse the situation to explain that you would like to be more aware and compassionate and that you need a few moments away to compose yourself.

When you strike out at another it is often because you are not feeling good inside about yourself. Recognize that when others create pain within you, when they seem to strike out at you, it is because they do not feel good inside about themselves either.

Learn to stop talking when the energy grows heavy and dense between you and another. If you can create physical distance, do so. You can then bring in light by sitting quietly, imagining peace. It may be difficult to imagine peace when you are feeling angry. Try imagining beautiful scenery, a good memory, or something that will restore a sense of balance. Then, invite your soul into your heart. Ask it to bring the highest consciousness possible into your loving being. You will begin to feel an intensification of peace and you may begin to feel sorry for what you have done or said. You may experience a sense that the whole issue got blown out of proportion, that you did not mean the things you said. Or, you may at this point be able to view the other person's anger or pain with compassion and detachment, not feeling personally responsible for his reaction.

*The more you understand
what you are learning from a situation,
the more rapidly you can leave it.*

Ask yourself what lessons you are learning from being with this person, or what growth you are accomplishing by being in this situation. Pain always signifies major opportunities for growth. Suppose, for instance, you are in pain because someone does not return your love to the degree you would like. It may be that you are learning to keep your heart open, no matter what the other person does. It may be that you are learning about humility, harmlessness and lack of self-importance. Grow quiet and ask your soul to show you the lessons; it will always respond. You will see that what has happened is a great gift even though at the time it may seem like a tragedy. Ask your soul to show you the gift. The degree to which you feel pain is often an indication of the size of the gift that awaits you when you understand why you set it up.

Understanding is not enough by itself, however. Once you begin to understand what you are to learn, it is important to act upon it. Some of you feel pain and separate from others when your love is not returned, or when you have pictures and expectations that are not met. Try not to make those people wrong; that can escalate a power struggle between you. You cannot find answers when you are in a power struggle. Instead, as you grow silent and calm your energy, imagine that you are embracing them with your heart, forgiving them no matter what.

Pain is a powerful indicator of growth, and it can be changed with love.

When you are in pain you are often closer to your soul than at any other time. As you learn to see energy and experience it more directly, the challenge will be to stay in your heart and focus upon what is higher and finer in others rather than what is lower. When you feel pain it is an indication that some area of your life is not working; some belief, thought, or emotion is crying out to be loved and healed. Do not make yourself wrong or think of yourself as a bad person, but see it as an opportunity to examine, experience, and heal that area of your life.

When people are angry with you, it is often an expression of their hurt. Most people feel that they only get angry with just cause, and only get hurt when someone lets them down, aggravates them, rejects them or makes unreasonable demands. But anger can also be used to control others. Is your fear of people's anger controlling your behavior around them? Do you use a threat of anger to control others?

When people get angry with you, or appear to want to hurt you, they may be doing it because they are in pain themselves. Because of their programs and upbringing, because of the way they look at the world, some people may think you have hurt them when you had no intention to do so. Sometimes people get angry when all you are doing is expressing an opinion that differs from theirs, or stating a preference of your own. Be sure you are not coming from a desire to control or manipulate, and if you are not, do not let their anger trigger pain within you.

I often see two people hurt when each only wanted the other's love. Often when people are hurt and in pain they really want you to put your arm around them and express gentleness, love, and understanding. How difficult it is to be gentle and loving when someone is acting in a way that creates pain or hurt inside you. It is part of learning to work with energy, however, to stop, soften your heart and listen when you are around hurt or angry energy. It is tempting to grow defensive, to get angry yourself, or to lash out at the people who are hurting you. You may feel that they are trying to put you down or make you wrong. Often separation comes from feeling defensive, feeling that you must protect your pride or dignity at all costs.

When you are in pain or hurt, what you really want from others is for them to listen to you, be gentle with you and understand that you are upset. You do not want them to withdraw and get defensive. You do not want them to get upset with you when you are angry, but instead to recognize that you have been hurt. Some of you yell at other people when you feel that they have hurt you. What you really want them to do is say "Yes, I see. I am sorry I hurt you."

*If others express anger with you,
or withhold their love in some way,
do not let their negativity
become a part of your response.*

When people are causing you pain, or are getting angry with you, realize that what they want from you is for you to love them. They do not want you to withdraw, get angry, feel hurt, or defend yourself. In truth, the issue rarely even matters to them. They are experiencing their own pain and it has nothing to do with you. Although they may blame it on you or tell you it is your fault, any pain they blame on you comes from a pain within them, from places within their hearts that are not yet open.

As you become more telepathic, you will be able to sense the pain in others even more, and that is why you will want to stay in your heart. As you view mankind from the higher realms, you will begin to see that there is much pain, anger and negativity. Yet, there is also much good.

As you begin to open to a greater awareness of the energy around you, you will also begin to open to an awareness of your own energy. You may see things in yourself that you want to change. It is important not to make wrong the things you see, for your soul will not continue to reveal them to you if you do. Instead, know that those areas are revealed to you so that you may begin to bring the light of consciousness and the love of your heart into them.

When people get angry at you, stand back. Realize that they do not know a better way to let go of their pain than to speak of it. If they are saying that you did something wrong, that you are bad, that you hurt them or caused them grief, do not attach yourself to their words. Realize that blaming others is the only way they know how to deal with the pain they feel. Do not think that you are responsible. They are responsible for their own upset or anger. You may have acted as a catalyst, but the pain had to be within them first. So, as they express their anger, do not start arguing or defending yourself; simply remain silent, hold open your heart and focus your love on them.

As they speak and get it all out, there may be a great temptation to jump in and tell them they are wrong, that you have not acted in such a manner as they are describing. Hold your tongue, for in the end, you will be grateful. Let them express their energy without putting anger out yourself. Once they have said it all you will still be in a loving and balanced space, feeling good about yourself. You will have mastered one of the most difficult of lessons—staying balanced around anger and pain.

If you have trouble forgiving people,
pretend the next time
you talk to them is
their last day on earth.

You would be able to come from your heart, no matter how the person acted. You would be generous, warm and loving. Perhaps a woman has caused you pain. Imagine as you go to see her again that it is her last day on earth. See how much you really appreciate her for who she is, the gifts she has given you, the love she has sent your way. See that it would be easy to let go of any pain and come from a high level if you knew this would be her last day. When you do see her again, pretend this meeting will be your last. Notice how you begin to see wonderful things about her—her light, being, and love. See how she had no real intention to hurt you, that she was acting from her own pain, confusion or lack of clarity. Perhaps you did something that pushed a button in her, and she is simply reacting, like a robot at times, to a program of pain within herself.

You *can* come from this high perspective. You can make every connection high and loving. Picture in your mind how you would act toward various people in your life if you knew you only had one more chance to be together. If you are not going to be with them again, send them a telepathic message that you absolutely forgive them, and send them love. Imagine that you have one day left to clear up any of the messages you have sent them. Even if they have pulled away and left you, there are telepathic messages still going on, and you can clear them up. If someone has died and left you, and there was anger between you, you can transmit forgiveness through your soul and it will reach theirs.

Release that pain within. Go to that peaceful, higher state. When you do connect, sit quietly with them, not rehashing the situation, not going into the details, but instead simply sitting in peace together. Tell them that you know they did not mean to hurt you, that you understand their position. Be loving, and the pain will disappear.

Even when you have decided to operate from a higher level and be more loving, you may not be able to do it for very long the first time you are with a person. Set a time limit in your mind that you think you can hold this higher energy. Perhaps you can maintain your new identity, or hold that focus of love for ten minutes or so. If you have been in a difficult situation with someone, do not arrange to spend four or five hours with him or her in this first attempt to be your new and higher self. Arrange for a brief contact, a length of time in which you know you can maintain and hold that higher focus. If you are living with this person, find things to do that keep you busy and away from their energy until you are ready to connect.

If you have fought with or experienced negative energy with someone, or have had someone withdraw from you, the next time you connect with the person do so in a way, and at a time and in a place, that will allow you to maintain that more loving perspective. When you sense that you are closing down, falling into anger or pain, find an excuse to leave. You will find that through practice this becomes easier, that you can hold a higher and higher focus with people for longer and longer periods of time, until you are naturally and automatically able to do so. You will gradually discover a new, more loving and higher you.

PLAYSHEET

1 | If there is a situation in your life right now that is causing you pain or hurt, if you feel angry at another or they are angry at you, write it here.

---

2 | Sit quietly, and invite in your soul. Fill your mind with peaceful thoughts. Imagine that you are rising to a higher, lighter, and more peaceful level. Ask your soul to show you what you have been learning from this situation. (See the other person as volunteering to act out this role to teach you something you need to learn.) Record your insights here.

3 | Imagine that the next time you see this person will be your last time together—possibly his or her last day on earth. Imagine also that you are the most secure, loving, compassionate, and wise person you know. What would you say to him or her that would heal the situation and create love between you?

XII

Opening Your Intuition

What is intuition, and how does it operate? Sometimes it is easier to explain intuition by saying what it is not. It is not the mind that figures everything out. It does not work like a computer going $a + b + c = d$. It does not utilize the principles of logic, as a computer does. Intuition is not ego; it does not operate in a world of form and structure.

Intuition is the ability to know without words, to sense the truth without explanations. Intuition operates beyond time and space; it is a link to your higher self. Intuition is not bound by the physical body. It operates knowing that past, present and future are simultaneous. It takes the desires of your conscious mind, goes out into the future and finds ways for you to have them. It speaks to you through insights, revelations and urges. It does not say to you as the intellect would, "I must do this tomorrow, this is on my list, this would be a good thing if I got it done." Instead, intuition says "Wouldn't it be fun, wouldn't it be joyful? This is what I want to do today." Often intuition feels like the playful child within you trying to lure you away from your hard work to the world of joy and play with its strong inner urges. Amazingly, in that playful world you can connect with all the answers you spent months working and trying to find.

Intuition can synthesize ideas in a flash. Geniuses like Edison and Einstein worked at a very refined and high level of intuition. They brought in their ideas from outside of time and space. Intuition goes beyond that which is known into the unknown. It can help you find answers and information that is not known in the mind of another person. Intuition, the sixth chakra, is associated with the color of indigo, red violet. If you find that you are attracted to that color it may be that you are opening in this area. For those of you who are opening the sixth chakra, or third eye as it has been called, the challenge is to hear your intuition, and then to follow it with action.

Many doorways will open when you follow your intuition.

You can find answers in a second to problems you have been working on for years. Say you want to leave a job and your intellect keeps saying "If you leave you'll starve, there is not enough money, you can't do it." Meanwhile your intuition is saying "Well, why don't you pretend you can do it—maybe there is a miracle or two out there that will make it happen." To bridge the gap between intellect and intuition, use the heart energy of trust and faith. Intuition will often give you answers that do not seem logical, yet the answers work if you trust them and act upon them.

How can you develop your intuition? First, learn to trust it. All of you hear whispers, have ideas in your mind about what you would like to do and be. You do have a vision of a more fulfilling life for yourself, although some of you do not allow yourself to fantasize about that vision very often, and even fewer of you trust it enough to bring it into your daily experience.

There are some traps in living too much in the world of intuition. One is that intuition operates in future time and you can be dazzled by future ideas, so that the present, in contrast, seems mundane and boring. There is a difference between physical reality and mental reality. The physical world is composed of much slower energy than the world of intuition, or the world of your thoughts. With intuition and your mind, you can conceive of an idea, carry it all the way through to fruition, and live it in a flash. Carrying it through in physical reality is much more time consuming, for the world of physical reality involves form and time. It can be much more fun to think about ideas than to actually create them. If you want to translate your intuition into physical reality, develop the qualities of patience, trust, confidence, focus and concentration.

All of you have the ability to use your intuition and follow your hunches. Sometimes you know who is going to be on the phone when it rings. That is intuition. You also have a vision of who you want to be. The challenge is to pay attention to that vision, to match it with your actions, words, attitudes and behavior. You will feel your true power when you act upon your intuition.

Acting on your intuition brings your goals to you faster.

If you exist on the intellectual level, you probably have lists of things you should do. (Listen to that word "should.") You most likely have your day, week, and month planned. Yet you wonder why you do not feel joyful and free. You may be living too much in the world of the intellect. Intellect and intuition have also been called the left brain and right brain. The left brain is the part of you that memorizes, deals with logic, and thinks in a time-oriented, sequential manner. The right brain is intuition and feelings, creativity and imagination; the world beyond words.

It is not enough to live in the world of intuition, for a person who lives there will do nothing with his life other than daydream and fantasize, and perhaps talk big. You have all seen those people who talk on and on of their big visions and plans and yet live in poverty and have not created anything. It takes much focus, patience, will and intent to bring intuition into reality. In physical reality, the minute you conceive of an idea, it is already old. That is why it is important to honor those things you have worked on in the past, to love yourself in the past. Everything is instantly in the past the minute it comes through your intuition into consciousness, the minute you hear it. Honor who you were and where you have come from; honor and love your past.

Many of you have a tendency to put yourself down for who you were. If you are writing a book, for instance, you may not like what you wrote a year ago. If you are in a career that is moving upward, you may look back and say "I was only a _____ two or three years ago." The more you can honor your past self, the more quickly you will be able to hear the voice of your intuition and move into your future. It is difficult to hear your intuition if you do not love who you were, for intuition opens to the degree to which you can love those forms you developed in the past. The more you love what you call into being the more you can operate at a higher level of intuition.

Send loving energy into your past.

It is important to go back and clean up your memories, for often the ego will bring you unwarted negative memories of the past that will hold you back. See the soul qualities you were developing during painful times and see that you were doing the best you knew how to do. The insights, skills and attitudes you have today were developed during those times.

Each lesson left you with the growth that made the next step possible. How often do you think of the wonderful things you have accomplished? You already have memories of successfully doing anything you want to accomplish; thinking of them will help you achieve success now. If you do not have the exact memory, you do have enough similar experiences, which, when put together, can help you.

If you want to make the visions of your intuition real you must first capture its images, slow them down, hold them in your mind, and then be patient enough to carry them out in action. The moment you capture your intuition, its vision becomes a memory, and thus becomes the past. It is important to remember the past with positive thoughts for it contains the visions you are bringing into reality now.

Think back to the "should do" lists made by your intellect. You can spend weeks and months, even years, trying to map out your future at the mental level, thinking every step through. It is valuable to have a plan in that it gives you the faith and belief that you can achieve your goals. The most important thing is to hold a steady vision of your goals. If you follow the plan too rigidly, you deny the miracles and the creative flow of energy within you. It is always faster and easier to create what you want by following your intuition. It can bring you, in its playfulness, all the goals and visions of your intellect, and usually even more. Intuition will often say, "Let's not do anything today, let's take a walk, let's go to the woods, let's go to the bookstore, let's indulge in something very unproductive." Then, lo and behold, you have produced more towards your higher goals at the end of the day than you would have by doing everything on your list. Perhaps you found an idea that took you six months ahead of your goals—for intuition lives in the future.

Many of you would prefer to be in the future rather than in the present or the past. But remember, it is one thing to live in the future and bring back visions to present time and another to never act upon those visions. If you do not act upon your visions you will not be able to create the life you want.

The best way to open your intuition is to listen to it.

How many of you have been hearing whispers in your mind that you have been ignoring? For instance, how many of you have heard whispers of what you would like to do for a career, but constantly create reasons why you can't do it? Would it not be simpler to create reasons why you can? It takes far more energy to hold yourself back than to allow yourself to move forward. Think how drained you feel when you dwell on the negative, and how energized you feel—and how easily things move—when you dwell on the positive.

You may really want to quit your job and pursue a hobby or longtime interest. You may find your mind whispering to you that it will work. You may hear of other people succeeding in your field, and find all kinds of indications from the universe that this is the right way to go. Intuition beckons you to the future with things you feel drawn to because you love them. When you follow that voice you will find doors opening everywhere. If you are finding closed doors, it is the universe telling you there is a better way to go. Don't keep pushing against closed doors; look around for the open ones.

Intuition talks to you in present time. Through urges, flashes of ideas, insights and feelings, intuition moves you in certain directions. To hear it, pay attention to your inner world of ideas and feelings. If you are forcing yourself to do one thing while your feelings are urging you to do something else, you are not paying attention to your intuition. Your intuition sends you messages constantly, telling you every moment what to do to open your energy. It is always directing you towards aliveness and a higher path.

Your intellect may often do battle with your intuition. You have been taught to honor your intellect, through your culture, through science, and through the academic world which is oriented to developing the rational, logical mind. Yet many of your greatest inventions—radio, electric lights, television—have come from a synthesis of intellect and intuition. The intellect can be highly developed; it loves to run the show. It can also feel threatened by intuition. Many of you have beliefs that say "if it happens too easily, it isn't right." Or, "if I don't work hard at it, the results aren't valuable." That is one way intellect can control.

When you operate from intuition things always happen easily.

Your intellect loves to plan everything out in a logical way; your intuition is spontaneous. Being flexible is important. If you rigidly stick to your pre-planned goals, you may miss many messages from your intuition telling you how to make things simpler. If you find yourself resisting doing something, stop and ask yourself what you would rather do instead. It may be that it is not the highest way to go or it may be the wrong time. If you trust and act upon your feelings from moment to moment, you will be flowing with your intuition and the universe.

There is a role for intellect, and that is to formulate plans, to decide where to go, and to carry things out with action. Intellect is like the captain of a ship, consulting maps, making plans and steering the ship. Yet the weather and the ocean actually determine the course; the captain must remain flexible and use his plans as a guideline. So it is with the intellect that steers your ship. Intuition tells you of storms ahead, of detours (that turn out to be shortcuts); it monitors a future path designed to bring you your highest good. Use your intellect to set goals, to aim you higher. Focus your will and intent on going higher—that is the best use of your intellect, to keep you on course, to set goals and to interact with the world. Your intuition will take you there the best, fastest and easiest way—if you follow your feelings, hunches, inner urges, and deeper desires.

For example, take the person who wants a new career. If he let go and kept picturing it, intuition would guide him to it. One day, while following a playful urge to go walking, he might run into a person or come up with an idea that would provide a starting point. Intellect may try to build a path logically, and not see any way things could work. It takes a great deal of trust to follow your feelings and intuition, for intuition usually shows you only one step at a time.

You can open your intuition by learning to listen to your feelings and act upon them. When you have an urge to do something, do it. Don't force yourself to go to a job you don't like—listen to your feelings. Begin to open to new ways to earn a living. To act upon your feelings may take a leap of faith. Look back at all the times you have listened to those inner urges, acted upon them and were amazed at your success.

Following your intuition requires a great deal of trust and faith. To develop that quality further you can go back and remember times when you believed in yourself, heard the whispers and acted upon them. Acting upon intuition requires flexibility and spontaneity. To develop those qualities you can remember times in which you were flexible, and let go of your plans, and things worked out even better than you expected. If you want to increase productivity, allow yourself to listen to your whispers and to act upon them. Allow yourself to play. Do those things you have been wanting to do. Be a child again. Create fun in your life and you will find that your creative energy will awaken and flow as never before.

PLAYSHEET

1 | Write down three times you followed your intuition in
the past—perhaps acting on a feeling, hunch, or
urge—and things turned out well:

- Creating my own business!
-

2 | Write down at least three things your mind has been
whispering—or maybe even shouting—to you to do.
These could be small or big things.

3 | Think of one step you could take towards each to bring it into your life.

4 | Mark your calendar with a date when you will take this step.

XIII

Your Mind,
Inner Dialogue, and
Personal Broadcast

Your mind puts out a powerful broadcast of energy. It also determines how you experience the world and what you create. Your thoughts are magnetic; they go out from you and draw to you those things you think about. Your inner dialogue is important, for the way you speak to yourself determines the events, people and objects you attract.

To become lighter, to create happier events in your life, it is important to use higher words and thoughts when you speak to yourself or others. Your thoughts create reality; they go out into the world and affect other people. As you move into the higher realms of energy, you will want to raise your thoughts by increasing their quality. As you begin thinking purer, kinder and more loving thoughts, you will begin to change the magnetism of your body and resonate with the higher planes of the universe.

You can begin by watching your inner dialogue. Do you make yourself wrong frequently? Do you tell yourself that your efforts are not enough? Are you always trying to rush, to hurry up, to make self-imposed and unreasonable deadlines? Are you always trying to please other people, telling yourself that if anyone is unhappy it's your fault and you have failed? Are you critical, finding fault with things rather than seeing the good, looking for what is not working and not right? Do you focus on what is missing and wrong or on what is working and going well?

Learning to control your inner dialogue is learning to make your mind obey rather than control you. It is learning to be able to choose what thoughts come into your mind, rather than be ruled by the thoughts that randomly pop up. Part of the goal of evolution is to bring the mind into the dominion of the soul. By watching your inner dialogue, loving yourself and forgiving yourself for all your mistakes (which are best viewed as learning experiences), you raise the level of your thinking. Notice what words you use and how you feel as you say them.

*Saying high, loving words
over and over raises
your mind's vibration.*

If you cannot focus for a long period of time on a certain thought, do not worry. It takes many years of on-going observation and intent to bring the mind to a point of stillness and focus. Each time you succeed in focusing on higher ideals and thoughts for even a moment or two, congratulate yourself. Whenever you think of it, remember to turn your attention to higher thoughts. Look for words that make you feel good when you say them to yourself.

If you notice yourself feeling anxious or depressed, use positive words to raise your energy. These are the words of the soul. You do not have to make them into statements. Say words to yourself such as LOVE, CLARITY, WILL, INTENT. Say I AM STRONG, GIVING, CARING, COMMITTED, ABUNDANT, RADIANT, LIGHT, ENTHUSIASTIC, PEACEFUL, TRANQUIL, SERENE. Think of all the beautiful, inspiring words you know. You do not need to make them into statements for these words to reach the deeper parts of your being. When you say the word peace, you open to the vibration of peace that exists in millions of minds throughout the world. You connect with peaceful thoughts and events, for the outer world has much peaceful energy you can tune into. Use positive, high words when you speak to yourself, words such as EFFORTLESS, INSPIRED, and CREATIVE. Make conscious use of these higher words. If you are feeling bad, simply say them over and over and you will begin to change your thoughts.

When you speak to yourself, use words that indicate present tense. Instead of saying, "Someday I will;" say, "I am now." The mind interprets what you say to yourself literally. If you say, "I will be happy," your mind takes that literally and creates what you want not as an event you experience *now*, but as something that will happen in the *future*. (Which means you will never experience it.) Watch that you do not put what you want now into future tense; instead speak of it as something you already have: "I love myself as I am today. I am happy today. I have money now. I have my soul-mate now." It may not appear to be true as you say it, but it will be shortly.

If you say, "I am not enough," your mind takes that statement and begins to create outer events in which you experience yourself as not enough. Imagine that 40,000 to 50,000 thoughts go through your mind every day. If you can turn even 2,000 of them into thoughts of light, love, abundance, and joy, you will rapidly change what you experience Within a month your experience of your life will be very different. It does not take that many high and loving thoughts to change your experience, for high and loving thoughts are many times more powerful than thoughts of a lower nature.

Talk of the qualities you aspire to as if you already have them.

If you aspire to be organized, start saying, "I am now organized" (rather than "I am going to be organized"). As you use higher words, you change your aura, emotions, and the health of your physical body. Not only do you feel better, you begin to tune into other people who carry those same higher thoughts and to create events in your life that are more abundant, loving, joyful and peaceful.

Watch when you use the words should, have to, and must. Do you frequently talk to yourself with these words? They often set up rebellion and create the opposite of their intent. Do you speak to yourself in a way that sounds like an angry parent, or do you have a loving voice within that permits you to flow with your own energy? When you catch yourself telling yourself you have to do something, see if you can change to something more permitting and gentle—a suggestion, rather than a command.

Working with your mind is like taming a wild horse. At first your mind may rebel. As you try to learn to focus, your mind may sidetrack you, thinking of anything but what you want. As you bring your mind more under the guidance of your soul, you will realize that your thoughts contribute to or hinder everyone around you, depending upon what you think of. The thoughts you send out can work for or against you and other people. Imagine that you are speaking of someone who is not present, criticizing him for his faults. Realize that even though the person is not there, he can hear telepathically what you are saying. He may not know it comes from you, but he will feel less powerful and worse about who he is. You will also pull to yourself criticism from other people who think of you.

You can raise the energy of the people around you or depress it by the thoughts you put into your mind. As you grow in your ability to sense energy, so do you grow in your ability to affect it. Thought involves very subtle energies. You can be obscure and unknown, or famous, and have just as much effect upon mankind. Many great beings choose to live anonymous lives. You may feel that you are very special, have an important mission, and yet feel you are not doing anything with your life that matches that feeling. There is a mass thought that having a great mission means you must become famous. Many highly evolved souls with much important work to do choose to do it anonymously. Maybe your work involves a small circle of friends or raising a family. You cannot know the worth of the work you are doing here on earth if you are judging it by the standards of your personality (which only looks at the form of it) and other people's or society's standards. Only through the eyes of your soul can you know the impact of your life on mankind.

By *evolving yourself to the highest level you can, you create a doorway for those one step behind you to come through.*

Much of the great work done for mankind is done in the telepathic arena, creating thoughts of a high vibration, and does not involve public recognition. Every being that evolves to his or her next level makes it that much easier for those just one step behind to follow. As you hold higher thoughts, learn your lessons, and radiate more love and peace, you are making a valuable contribution to mankind. Through those lines of thought that radiate out from you, you affect many people. Do not think that to have great effect upon people you must be famous, be on TV, or write books. Some people are learning about certain fields so that as they tap into the universal mind they open that doorway for mankind. Every place you create higher, wiser and more loving thoughts you have made a contribution.

There are those who hold a great vision of peace for the planet so that when people think of peace they will be able to tune in to a vision of it. They live very solitary lives, and are very gentle and loving beings, virtually anonymous and living alone, often in isolated areas. All they do is hold the vision of peace so all who desire it may find those images telepathically available. Many of you are affecting the earth telepathically through your own personal broadcast in ways you cannot know.

Your thoughts are like a magnet. Not only does the level of your thoughts determine what you attract, it determines what you affect. As you think higher thoughts, you begin to connect with the higher forces and places in the universe. As your mind creates an affinity with the higher planes, you begin to attract greater and greater light into your life. When you have darker thoughts of pain or fear, you attract like thoughts from the universe and you may find it more difficult to reach upward, for you connect with people who operate at a lower level.

Although your thoughts create reality, until you have reached a certain level of self-love and mental mastery there is a veil between your thoughts and their ability to manifest. You may have wondered why your thoughts don't seem to always be able to create what you want. For instance, you may be picturing your body thin and yet it is not responding. You are wondering why your thoughts are not manifesting a thinner reality. However, if you do not have many loving thoughts about your body, you would not want every thought about your body to manifest instantly. There will be a veil between the thought and the creation of it in that particular area until your thoughts about that area are brought up to a higher level. If you want to change this, you can learn to think about your body in a more loving way. Notice if you are putting your body down, if you have unloving thoughts about it, and change them to thoughts of acceptance. As you change all of your thoughts about your body into more loving and accepting ones, it becomes possible to create the thinner body you are picturing, for your negative pictures are no longer present to create potential damage.

You would not be able to handle it if every thought you had was created instantly. Your life would change too quickly. Your home would be different from day to day. Your world could not function if everything changed with the rapidity of your thoughts. So you have created a veil that stands between you and manifesting your thoughts. You will be able to manifest your thoughts more quickly in the areas where they are loving and high. If you have not mastered the unloving thoughts in an area, it would be too destructive to manifest your thoughts in that area instantly. If you are trying to get something and it is not coming, look at all of the thoughts you are having about that area of your life, and substitute thoughts of a higher quality for any negative thoughts you discover.

You have mental ties in every direction, in what has been called a "Mental Brotherhood" of men. One goal of your soul is to bring your mind into a higher, more loving vibration. To do this, you want to receive thoughts not from men, but from the higher levels of reality. If you are idly thinking of other people, you draw in whatever feeling they have or whatever level of thought they carry at that time. If they are in pain, you draw it in. That is why it is important when you think of other people to send them love, for when you are sending love you cannot pick up their broadcast. If you notice people coming into your mind, send them love and let them go; do not dwell on their situation or what is happening in their lives, for as you do so you begin to bring their reality into your own.

You CAN control your thoughts.

You can train your mind to choose what you think, and not allow thoughts to come up randomly and hold you in their grip. The thoughts that are in the trained mind are there by invitation and choice. You can turn away negative thoughts, saying no to them over and over. You can learn to substitute higher thoughts and words. You can learn to refrain from thinking those things you do not want to think.

There are several techniques you can use to train your mind. One is to take an object such as a flower, crystal or candle, and spend a full minute focusing on it. If any other thoughts come into your mind, simply imagine them floating away as you continue to focus on the object. By not letting your mind wander, you are training it to think of what you are directing it to think of. Do it for fun. See how long you can direct your mind to think about what you want it to. See if you can increase the length of time you hold that focus steady from one minute to five.

The next step is to look at the same object, then close your eyes and recreate it in your mind in perfect detail—the color, the texture, the essence of the object.

This helps you become more observant, and helps you train your mind to be more accurate in what it sees inside, for often you see one thing and your mind tells you you saw something else. It also develops your ability to hold an image steady in your mind. Go back and forth, opening and closing your eyes, until you can "feel" the flower or object as if it were as real inside as when viewed with your eyes. This exercise will help you learn to make what you "see" inside your mind real in the outer world. If you determine that you will see beauty around you, and begin to observe what is beautiful, holding those images clearly inside, you will soon see beauty everywhere, even where you did not see or experience it before.

A *trained mind creates*
emotional calm and inner peace
by focusing on higher ideals,
wisdom, and love.

Exhaust to do

Another way to train your mind is to simply observe for a period of time, one to five minutes, the flow of thoughts as they pass through you. An untrained mind tends to find its attention caught by anything that comes its way. It is led by the attractions and impulses of the moment, by the cues from the universe and those things that come and go. Watch the flow of your thoughts—for many thoughts are triggered by outer-directed stimuli such as phone calls, TV, and the people you are around. Thoughts of other people and telepathic connections can trigger the mind also. The goal is to learn to become inner-directed, so that you decide what you want to think about rather than having your thoughts determined by what is happening around you. The untrained mind leads the emotions up and down according to the thoughts that march through.

Mental chatter needs to be calmed down before you can receive higher information. If you can stop that chatter for a second, feeling an inner sense of calm, having no thoughts, you create an opening for a higher vibration to come through. Practice putting different thoughts into your mind. Gain a sense that your thoughts are not you but are often products of internal chatter.

Your mind is like a fine set of antennae extending outward in all directions. Thoughts come and go rapidly and are often triggered by sources outside yourself, until you begin to bring them under the control and direction of your soul. Notice how you suddenly think about something out of the clear blue sky; it is often because you are picking up thoughts from people you are connected to. You need to stop responding automatically to your own thoughts, and thus to the thoughts of others. You can begin to do so by turning your thoughts upward, by watching your inner dialogue, and constantly substituting fine, high and loving thoughts for any that are not as high as you would like.

You can change the energy between yourself and anyone by using positive words.

Another exercise to train your mind can be done for fun with your friends and those people you connect with. Notice as they talk to you, whether they are talking in past, present or future time. Do they use words that uplift you, or do they use words and thoughts that strike chords in your lower self? Interject words in the conversation that are higher and lighter. You can feel your own brightness increasing, your own sense of joy growing larger as you speak words of encouragement. If you would like to bring their energy up, say words that are high and loving and watch the change in their energy and yours. As you say these words, you heal yourself and keep from tuning in to the telepathic communication at lower levels from other people.

You will begin to resonate with the thousands of minds that are thinking at these higher levels. You will find yourself becoming stronger and clearer. If you hear someone saying something such as "the world is a very *frightening* place," and you do not want that to be a part of your reality, mentally substitute different words, such as "the world is a very *joyful* place." You can use your mind to cancel out the negative words you hear from others, replacing them with higher, finer and more loving thoughts. You will find that you make a different mirror, a reflection of a higher plane, available to others as well. Be aware that if you use this process you may feel so light and joyful to other people you will be sought after as popular company.

When you are with people, see if you can turn off your thoughts, even for a few moments. Do not react, judge or make any mental comments to yourself about what they are saying. Do not think about ways you can help them; do not think of responses, but listen with a silent mind. You will begin to pick up much beneath the surface of what they are saying, such as feelings, images and pictures. Do this with a sense of play and joy.

You can master your thoughts, your inner dialogue and your personal broadcast. Over and over, decline negative thoughts that come into your mind. Substitute higher ones. Fix your mind on higher ideas no matter what is going on around you. Spend some time learning to hold a focus, taming your mind and harnessing it as your friend. As you do so, you will become a source of light and love for all around you.

PLAYSHEET

1 | Take the alphabet and think of the highest word or words you can for each letter.

A bundance	J oyful	R elaxed
B lessings	K	S trong
C harm	L ove	T ough
D eliverance	M oney	U
E nlighted	N	V igor
F ree	O pen	W onder
G orgeous	P leasing	X
H ome	Q ueen	Y osemite
I ndependent		Z orth

2 | Notice how you feel after writing out these high and positive words. A game to play while you are driving—look at car license plates, and create high words out of the letters you see.

3 | Find an object such as a flower or crystal. Spend a full minute focusing on it, letting go of any thoughts that come into your mind. Notice how hard or easy it was to keep your mind focused for that length of time.

4 | Take this same object and see if you can close your eyes and remember it exactly.

XIV

Wisdom: Being
Your Higher Self

As you become aware of the energy around you, wisdom helps you understand it. You begin seeing that everything that happens to you is meant to assist you in going even higher. As you begin to believe that all things are being created for your highest good, it becomes so. Your positive perspective creates a supportive and nurturing environment around you; it allows energy to flow with you, rather than against you.

Wisdom is the ability to be conscious of what is happening around you, to see the higher truth, and express yourself with compassion. It makes the universe around you friendly rather than hostile. Believing that everything is happening for your good renders negative energy harmless.

When you act from wisdom, you feel good inside. You know that you have stopped for a moment, taken the time to reflect, and reached upward for your direction. What you then create is from that higher space. You have demonstrated wisdom many times. Use your memories of the past to fill your consciousness with visions of yourself as a wise person, rather than to remember the times you were not wise.

As you become more aware of energy, you will begin to sense people's thoughts and feelings to one degree or another. As you open to energy, you will begin to get more input and information from the universe. Wisdom helps you to soften that information, to reinterpret the messages. The way you view the world around you is the way you will experience it. Rather than thinking, "Everything is going against me," or "It's unfortunate that this happened," look at events from a higher perspective and realize that everything happening to you can be seen as a good thing. This is the wisdom of your soul, for your soul is always trying to help you see your life in a higher way.

Feeling love rather than judgment changes negative energy into harmless energy.

Wisdom comes from the heart. The wise heart embraces others with a feeling of compassion for whatever stage they are at in their souls' evolution; it approaches them with a feeling of love and oneness rather than judgment. The wise man knows that when he feels separate from those less evolved he also separates himself from those who are more evolved, and thus delays his own journey upward. Through the eyes of love, all energy becomes more beautiful.

Wisdom is the ability to know what is important in your life and what is not, what things are distractions and what things are the call of your soul. It is the ability to sort through all the data that is coming in and select only those things that contribute to your sense of well-being. There may be something you want to accomplish and yet you never have the time; you keep getting distracted by housework, phone calls, demands of other people. Wisdom is the ability to know which activities are truly serving your higher purpose and which are merely distractions from your path. You can make the people, thoughts and events in your life positive, nurturing, and supportive. You can create a personal environment that is beneficial to you, rather than harmful.

Wisdom is understanding your mind and how it works. Your mind is a magnificent tool for learning. Because it wants to keep you motivated to learn more, it is never satisfied. No matter what you do, your mind is always wanting to move on to the next thing. If you identify with your mind you will feel unfulfilled and unsatisfied. As you identify with your deeper being, your soul, you will achieve feelings of inner contentment and peace. The deeper being is the part of you that experiences your feelings and chooses what thoughts to have.

R*ather than resisting or
getting rid of lower thoughts,
simply place thoughts of a
higher nature by their side.*

Whatever you picture you will get. Part of growth is choosing to picture higher things. Learn to identify "you" as the deeper part of your being, the part that chooses what thoughts to put in your mind, that selects emotions and reactions and desires. As you evolve, you will work with your mind to hold high and positive thoughts. Even when beset by troubles, people with trained minds can stay away from the temptation of anxiety or anger by knowing that nothing stays in their minds that is not there by their choice and invitation.

When you are angry at someone, you can either express it or release it. Expressing anger, putting it out to the world verbally, always looking out to make sure no one takes advantage of you, telling people that they make you angry, will only attract more of what you are trying to avoid. If you release anger, you no longer have it in you and you will not draw more to you. When you release those things that make you angry or sad or guilty, you no longer attract them to you. You *can* choose to release things without expressing anger, for you are a fully participating individual in everything that happens to you.

You may feel you don't have as much control as you would like over the things that happen to you, but you *can* control your response to them. You can choose how you want to react. You can select those responses which allow you to feel good. Rather than express anger, release it. Rather than express hatred, release it. Then another's anger or hatred cannot attach to you, for there is no place within you that it will stick to. Be generous with your forgiveness, for it is a response to anger that allows you to rise above it.

Wisdom is being able to discern which messages to pay attention to and which to release.

When people speak to you in anger, saying unkind or untrue things, it is best to learn to forgive them. It is wise to learn not to respond to the negativity or fear in others. Keep your heart open and come from that loving, compassionate and higher view. There are many who would speak of hard times, who blame others, and create bad feelings through their words and their anger. Learn not to respond with anger but to focus instead on other things.

Do not take offense, for offense taken is as bad as offense given. When you take offense, you contribute to negative energy, and thus there is negative energy around you that can attract more of the same. When you get offended, you close down your heart and thus turn away from your connection to your soul. Do not get offended when people speak from anger or fear, for it is coming from a lesser self. Learn to focus on their greater selves, for whatever you focus on and pay attention to is what you draw out in the people around you.

As you focus on the greatness in others, you will attract higher thoughts about yourself from other people. See them as doing the best they know how. It is important to notice when people do not speak to you from their higher selves. Respond to them with compassion, as you would respond to a small child who did not know any better. Forgive them and let it go. People cannot hurt you; only you can choose to hurt yourself by your response to them. This gives you the ultimate power to control the world you experience. If you are able to choose your response, you can choose to feel joy and peace, and thus change your world.

Learn to ignore the trivial and unimportant, so that when you speak of those things that are important, you will be heard. Learn to accept those things that do not matter, so that you will be able to pay attention to those that do. Train your focus and awareness to acknowledge beauty and harmony, so that you see the good and the wise. Turn your antennae in the direction of what is supportive and nurturing.

What is loving to the self is always loving to others.

Learn to know the difference between your wishes and the wishes of others. You can acquire the ability to choose what is right for you by checking in with your higher self. If you find a feeling of heaviness or resistance, take time to look deeper. What is right for you will also be right for other people. Have you ever forced yourself to go somewhere with someone because you felt obligated, only to discover the other person didn't really want to be there either? Have you ever cancelled an appointment and found that the other person was getting ready to call you to do the same?

Allow yourself to choose which energies you want to feel and be a part of and which energies you simply want to release and let go of. You may be having many experiences right now in which others want something from you, or are disappointed in you, or are accusing you of not living up to what they expect. Wisdom is learning what is yours—your thoughts, your expectations—and what is another person's.

How do you tell what energy is yours and what is others'? Often you cannot tell until you "wear" their energy. For instance, when you live with a person, and he feels strongly about a moral issue, you may find yourself taking the same view. Then, when you separate, you discover that you feel differently about that issue. You have "worn" someone else's beliefs for a while. Frequently you cannot know if a desire is yours or not until you try it. You may discover that you love to think that way, or you may discover that you do not.

From time to time in the process of growth, you will bring other people's energy into your life; you will try living by their rules, principles and values to discover if they are yours. You may choose to keep those that agree with you. It will be your challenge to let go of those that do not. Do not feel guilty if you find yourself rejecting another's views or beliefs, even when those beliefs seem to be very moral or fit with what people call "right." Only you can know what is right for yourself. It is the same with all energy you perceive in the universe; if it does not work for you then you do not need to keep it.

Wisdom is the ability to know when to act and when not to.

Wisdom is not the mind, although it includes the mind. Your mind gathers all the facts and tries to make decisions based upon known data. Wisdom comes from combining what is intuitively known, the gut-level feeling, with what is intellectually known. It helps you to know which impulses come from your lower nature and which come from your higher self.

Often your mind presents you with many ideas. More opportunities may come to you than you can possibly act upon. Do not make yourself wrong if you can't seem to bring yourself to act upon what seems to be a golden opportunity. Follow that deeper note of understanding that says in a whisper "wait." If your mind is telling you to wait but that inner voice says act, take a leap of faith, dare to take a risk—then do so.

You might ask how a great master would demonstrate wisdom. He would know when to be strict and stern, and when to be loving and generous. Not always is it wise to give people what they think they need. Small children may think they need an unlimited supply of candy to be happy; you, with a higher view, can see that good nutrition will serve them better in the long run. Sometimes it is necessary to hold a higher vision for others and assist them in seeing it rather than giving them what they are asking for. You may even need to deny them something they think they need. People who have a great deal of money have discovered that giving people money does *not* solve all their problems; in fact, it often creates more trouble. You may have enough money to lend relatives in need, but from your wise self you know that they have created a lack of money to learn from. You may be of more assistance to them by helping them discover their higher purpose and encouraging them to do what they love than by giving them money, which will last a short while but will not help in the long run. Indeed, when they run out you are in the same spot. Wisdom is knowing how to teach people to fish, rather than giving them fish.

It is knowing when to help and when not to. For instance, watching children learn a new skill, it is tempting to jump in and show them how to do it better. Yet, they cannot learn unless they try it themselves, however good or bad the effort. You must stand by quietly, in your wisdom, and let them learn by trial and error. It is the same with friends and loved ones in your life. Often, the most loving thing you can do for people is to stand by while they learn their lessons. If you come in and act as their savior, you may take away the lessons and growth they were getting out of that situation. Then they will have to create it all over again. You can assist them more by focusing light on them, and by helping them recognize what they are learning from the situation. It may feel hard to be wise, for often it is easier to jump in and rescue people than stand by and watch them go through difficult and sometimes painful lessons.

It *is important*
to experience compassion
rather than sympathy.

Sympathy is feeling sorry for others, seeing that what is happening to them is negative or bad. Compassion is seeing that what is happening to them is for their growth, and assisting them in seeing that also. Compassion reframes an experience they may perceive as unfortunate or bad into something they can understand. Realize that when you feel sympathy for people, you begin to vibrate with them and take their lower energy into yourself. When you come from compassion, you do not bring in their negativity.

Being firm with people may not be easy but it can be a greater gift than being the nice guy all the time. You have experienced friends to whom you give and give, who do not seem to appreciate what you do. If your offers of help are doing no apparent good, it is time to put your energy elsewhere. You may risk not being liked in the short run, but in the long run you will gain from following this higher wisdom.

One of the greatest gifts you give others is precise, accurate and compassionate communication of the truth. It takes a great deal of wisdom to know what to say and when to say it. If you are in doubt about saying something to someone, get silent and go within. If it feels like your communication will serve him in his growth, then say it. If it feels like it will fall on deaf ears or he will resist it, keep it to yourself. If you are speaking out of a desire for personal gain, to get him to do something you want him to do, it is better to remain silent. Personal gain cannot be the motivation if you are truly to help. There is power in silence, and there is power in communication given at the right time.

Stop before you speak and reflect, "Does this communication serve this person's highest vision?" Then you are coming from wisdom. A wise person chooses words with precision when he speaks. He asks before he communicates to others, "How does what I say serve their growth?" If it does not serve the other person in any way, he does not say it. Whenever you put out high and wise energy, you draw it back to yourself.

Recognize the level of the soul you are with. Do not expect calculus from a second grader. Be gentle with those around you. Any negative energy sent your way is only coming from their fear; you do not need to react with fear. Can you imagine if you were only as open and loving as the people around you? The challenge is to use your innate wisdom to see all situations from a higher perspective, to release the energy you do not want, and to come from your own center of love and compassion, regardless of the level of love in the people around you.

Be the leader. Dare to be wise! Dare to be the one who is the most loving, compassionate, open and vulnerable. Set the example; do not wait for others to be open and wise first. You will soon discover the power of one open, wise, and loving person to transform the entire universe around him or her.

PLAYSHEET

1 | Sit quietly and relax. Think about the day and week ahead. What things are you planning to do that are truly important and what things are merely distractions that could be eliminated?

2 | Is there anything you plan to do in the next day or week that is an obligation or another's wish of you rather than your own?

3 | Think of someone in your life who wants something from you. Get quiet and bring in your wiser self. Is there anything you could give that person, besides what he *thinks* he needs, that would truly serve him or her?

4 | What is the most important thing you could accomplish today? Make the decision you will do it.

XV

Telepathy: Understanding Nonverbal Communication

There are two basic forms of communication, verbal and telepathic, or nonverbal. Each one of you has experienced telepathy. You receive telepathic messages emotionally or mentally. You are a walking broadcast station, and you pick up messages constantly from your community and friends. You have telepathic chords coming not only from people you know now, but from people you *will* know and those that you have known. You have many chords of energy coming in and out of you. They can be thought of as radio waves, linking you to others.

You can learn to turn down the volume, sever the ties, monitor what comes in and goes out, and transform negative energy into positive energy. The loudest broadcast you receive is from those you love and open your heart to; the faintest whispers usually come from those you knew years ago, or from distant friends. It is important to know how to control the volume, the frequency, and how you receive these messages, emotionally or mentally, for the quality of your telepathic connections determines whether your bonds will be positive and helpful or hinder you.

You are telepathically part of a larger community consisting of your neighborhood and your town. Communities have certain thoughtforms that are particular to them, and those thoughts are very real. Each community is a pocket of energy. You pick up the messages of your community from everywhere—restaurants, bookstores, grocery stores and food markets, even from the cars you drive past. Energy is experienced at a subtle level; telepathic messages come to you through the vibrations set off by the thoughts of people in your community. Every community has a unique blend of energies.

When you sit and eat in a restaurant you can pick up the feelings and thoughts of the people around you. All of you pick up the thoughtforms of your community and the thoughts and feelings of your neighbors. Telepathic reception is stronger the closer physically you are to people.

Be aware of the thoughtforms in your community.

Do you find that you feel better in a place other than where you live? Do you find that you like being one place and dislike being somewhere else? You may not be compatible with the thoughtforms of the neighborhood and the community you are in. Look at your neighbors, their age, belief systems, and reality, and you will begin to get an idea of the thoughtforms you live around.

The telepathic influences of those closest to you—loved ones and friends—are even stronger. All of you are both telepathic senders and receivers, to some degree. All communication and healing comes first from the telepathic sending and receiving of it. It is often followed by words, but underneath the words people speak are many nuances of feelings and pictures that are being transmitted telepathically.

Your mind is like a TV set with many channels. Coming in on one station, for instance, could be your husband, wife or partner. You may have a separate station for each friend. Many thousands of messages come at you all day. You can learn to choose which ones you will pick up.

Are you a victim of all those telepathic messages? Are you bound to have low energy because those around you have low energy? It depends upon your ability to turn the dial and select what you bring into yourself. Most of you experience telepathy on an emotional level, bringing in other people's emotions. It is far better to receive messages through your higher centers. You tend to bring in other people's feelings and think they are yours if you receive information emotionally. That is how many of you lose a sense of who you are.

Imagine you are sitting in an apartment, and the neighbors on one side have a loud radio playing rock and roll. The neighbors on the other side of you are playing very loud classical music. Your own TV is going in one room and you have a radio station playing in another. Neighbors above and below you are playing completely different music, and you also hear loud voices coming from all the different apartments. Imagine how hard it would be to get in touch with your own energy with all that noise going on. That is what most of you experience all day long. It is happening at a subconscious level, but the telepathic noise and chatter is there.

You can learn to decipher the messages, choosing which ones you want to listen to and which ones you don't. You can learn to stop receiving them emotionally and start receiving them in your higher self. You can learn how to use the telepathic messages around you for your and others' highest good.

Imagine walking into a room and finding that the person you have come to see is extremely tense and nervous. Suddenly you find yourself much more worried about your life, and much more tense about things in general. Most of you experience this frequently without even realizing you are picking up emotional telepathic energy. You may simply think, "I'm really jumpy." You may even be picking up messages on your way to places. Have you ever noticed as you go to see someone, that as you get closer you become very happy, or tired and unhappy, or anxious? All of these are examples of picking up emotional messages from others. The feelings seem like your own, until you learn to recognize them as coming from others.

> You cannot know
> what you are picking up telepathically
> until you know your own energy.

To become aware of your own energy, focus on yourself as you wake up in the morning. You feel different each morning, have different issues on your mind—people you are going to see, new things that will come up for you that day. As you wake up, you haven't yet begun picking up the telepathic transmissions from people you are going to see, and are the most aware of who you are. Ask, "How do I feel?" You may find you are waking up tense, or elated and happy. Focusing on your feelings as you wake up establishes a reference point you can use all day.

You may know that in the evening you are going to see someone, a loved one or a friend. You may be thinking of something you are going to do, or thinking of work you are doing on a project. You may be thinking about your job, family, or friends. As you telepathically tune into those people you will be associating with, you begin to pull in their energy. If you first experience your own feelings, then you can be aware of any changes in yourself when you are around other people. As you think of other people, note any changes in your energy. For instance, you wake up very happy, but as you think about going to work and dealing with a co-worker, you begin to feel tense and anxious. You notice that you are feeling depressed and irritated with your life. If you did not remember that you woke up feeling good, you might begin to think *you* are irritated or depressed. Having recognized how you felt as you woke up, you can see that you are picking up your co-worker's tension and irritability.

If you wonder how people feel about you, ask yourself how you feel when you think of them. If you aren't aware of how you felt when you woke up, or before you thought of them, you won't be able to experience the difference in yourself when you think of them. If you ponder on them and become sad, feel they don't want you, or become aware of a feeling of pressure, notice how those feelings compare to what you were feeling before you started thinking of them. You will then know, at a feeling level, how people are responding to you.

People are aware of your nonverbal communication with them at some level. If you are fighting telepathically with some people, saying to them, "I don't want you to treat me this way, I won't take it anymore, I won't do this or that," they are aware of what you are sending them and you may experience more struggle and resistance from them. They may not pick up your precise words. They may pick up your message only as a feeling from you, depending upon their ability to receive; they will pick it up emotionally and work with it on that level. Your message will feel bad to them, and when they tune into you they will most probably have an urge to pull away. If you are thinking intently about people who do not want to be aware of you, they always have the power to turn off receiving *your* thoughts of them. If you do not want them to pull away, then send them thoughts of loving acceptance. That always opens doors.

If you are spending hours reflecting on certain people, are they spending time thinking about you? You have the ability to know. If when you think of them you feel a sense of resistance or irritation from them, then they are not thinking of you and they find your thoughts an intrusion. If, on the other hand, you find it delightful to think about them and easy to fantasize about them, or have a warm feeling in your heart, then they are welcoming you to join them on the telepathic level.

You have the ability to know what others are thinking.

The first step is to get into a centered, relaxed feeling. You cannot clearly sense energy through intense emotions. If you want to know what another person is thinking, relax and calm yourself, and let your mind be as silent as possible. You may want to imagine you are in the other person's shoes, looking at yourself. Almost always, the underlying feeling you have when you think of others is the feeling they have when they think of you. If you are going back and forth about how you feel about them, then they are probably doing the same. The particular issues may not be identical, but the underlying feeling is something you can learn to trust.

If someone has not called you, for instance, and you have been waiting for him to connect with you, look at your own thoughts and feelings, for others pick up your thoughts and feelings when they think of you. If you have said to him in your mind, "I really don't like the way you are treating me and I don't want you in my life," that may be why he stopped calling you. Be aware that people *do* receive your telepathic messages, especially in a close relationship. When you send out firm decisions, they are immediately picked up by others. You can always feel when people are inviting you to join them telepathically. It is easy and pleasant to link with them mentally. You can send them messages and feel their presence without a heavy feeling in your heart. You can imagine what they are doing without feeling sad, depressed or pushed away.

When you send out emotional messages, you affect other people. What you broadcast is picked up by those that love and care about you. Mankind as a race is opening telepathically. This is the level where most healing takes place.

*You can gain control
over the telepathic messages
you send and receive.*

As you learn to control your sending and receiving of telepathic messages you will no longer be controlled by them. All of you are affected by others telepathically to some degree. You want to know what other people are thinking about you. You have the ability to know; you only need to learn how to tune in. The first way to free yourself from being affected emotionally by others is to wake up in the morning and sense your energy; then monitor it constantly throughout the day. After a while you will get used to checking your emotional states and thoughts often. At least once when you are with someone, pay attention to how you feel. Do you feel better or worse? Do you suddenly feel more troubled, anxious, or happier?

Learn to monitor yourself. When you take in emotional energy from other people telepathically you almost always experience it as if it were *your* energy. Knowing what *you* feel like, you can learn to recognize when others are affecting you. You will only learn through practice; there is no shortcut. When you are on your way to see someone, take note of your emotions, thoughts and the feelings in your physical body. As you walk or drive to the meeting, monitor how these things are changing. While you are together, check in again. Awareness of how you are being affected brings emotional energy from other people you may have let in up into your higher centers.

Many of you are looking for ways to connect with your higher self by developing your ability to tune into your inner guidance. Emotional messages of others and your own thought patterns can interfere. You can work with your thought patterns, which tend to seek more familiar ways of being than those required to think in new and higher ways. It takes a great deal of focus and intent to change thinking patterns. It is like beginning to exercise. You would not run five miles the first day you started; you would have to build up to it. Once you've learned to tune into and monitor your feelings you will have a clearer sense of how you are picking up energy from other people emotionally and mentally.

You receive telepathic messages in your emotional center from those who love you and those you love. Most people desire intimate connections, that kind of love in which two people are so linked that each anticipates what the other wants and needs, and is anticipated in turn. A fear of that deep bond, however, keeps many people from it. If you are not centered and aware of who you are, you cannot begin to join with another at that deeper level without losing yourself.

*If you want a deep.
intimate relationship with another,
first become aware of who you are.*

Are you happy today? Are you sad? For a moment, remember when you woke up this morning. Go all the way back and ask how you felt. Picture yourself moving through the day. Recapture some of your emotions; take a look at who you were with, and notice your changing emotional energy. Were you affected by other people you were with or thought about?

It is important to understand your emotional reception of energy, because as children you received the emotions of others and you were not taught how to stop, change, or transmute them. Most of you went through childhoods in which you did not know who you were. You were so open telepathically to the wishes, wants, and demands of others that you often thought that what they wanted was what you wanted. As a result, many of you are confused about your identity. All of you who desire to heal, counsel, or help others, professionally or just as friends, are very open telepathically.

Many of you grew up as very sensitive children, aware of how people around you were feeling, and bombarded with messages from all around. There are many unique problems associated with growing up as an intuitive, sensitive person. Many of you experienced extreme sensitivity, caring for other people's feelings almost more than your own, sensing another person's hurt as if you were hurt yourself, trying to protect others from feeling pain, loving others at a level you often found not returned. Growing up telepathically sensitive can mean hearing double messages from your parents and others—"No, I'm fine today, dear," when you sense sadness and tension. It can mean wondering how people can be cruel when you yourself cannot bear to hurt because you feel the pain in another, wondering if people are insensitive and cold, or if you are the only one who can perceive certain things around you.

For some of you it meant feeling you were somehow different from others. You may have felt as a child that you didn't fit in, and school with its social life was often hard. On the other hand, some of you used your sensitivity to fit right in and get what you wanted.

Many people are going through the problems associated with being telepathic today. It is important to understand that part of your inability to know who you are comes from the telepathic abilities that exist within you. Many of you have had experiences with telepathy, perhaps more than you would even want. The example I gave earlier of all the radio stations and all the TVs playing at once is how most of you had to deal with your childhood. You were picking up many demands from many people, and most of you tried hard to please. You could see that it was easier to give people what they wanted, though some of you rebelled and did the opposite if the demands went too much against who you were, or if it appeared they could never be satisfied. Many of you used anger and rebellion to block the telepathic control other people tried to exert over you.

Telepathy is a problem
when it is not understood,
and a gift and a responsibility when it is.

If you are telepathic, you can send messages as well as receive them. You have a responsibility to others in what you send out. Most of you receive and send from the emotional center, but you can also send with words, which moves your communication to the mental level. Almost everyone experiences emotional telepathy, but few experience mental telepathy. It is not something that makes you better or superior to others. Unless you learn about it, telepathy can be a problem as well as a gift. Being telepathic, you are able to pick up messages and send them out. Do you understand how you can affect others with this gift?

You have certain ways of thinking, patterns of thought, that occur throughout the day. Have you noticed when you are walking or riding that your mind automatically falls into certain patterns, reflecting perhaps on housework, mundane things, a problem, or something that you think of when you have nothing better to do? You have a responsibility to move these thoughts to a higher energy level, for others receive and are affected by them. To change these thought habits will require first a commitment to change, and then a conscious effort to bring them up to higher levels when you recognize their presence.

It is important to learn to concentrate and to focus your mind where you choose, thinking of higher ideals rather than the mundane. It doesn't matter that the things you do seem unimportant or minor; it is not the kind of work you do but the way in which you do it and how you think about it that determines your evolution. Practice controlling your thoughts of things that seem unimportant, and you will be prepared to watch your thoughts on the larger and more important things.

You may find yourself arguing with people in your mind, talking to them and getting mad at them. You may find yourself discussing things with them as if you truly

have a live conversation going on. Whatever you are sending out in words is being received by the other person. This
is mental rather than emotional telepathy. However, not
everyone has the ability to receive words as clearly as you
are sending them. Some people receive them as a feeling
from you. Others find themselves carrying on a mental
debate with you. You may notice that the next time you get
together it is as if you start verbally where you left off
mentally.

If you are telepathic, you have a responsibility—you
cannot pretend you don't know what is happening between you and another person. You do know at a deep
level and you can learn to bring that knowing to the light
of consciousness. You cannot avoid the responsibility of
what you send out either, for when you send anger, you
are sending it out to all those you know. You begin to
resonate with those people who are angry and you bring
their broadcasts into yourself. You may think that you are
sending your anger just to the person you are mad at, but
be aware that on the telepathic level it goes out into the
whole world. When you are loving and peaceful, you send
that energy out to others to use if they choose.

When you think of others
they receive energy from you.

I have been asked many times, "When I think of people,
does that mean they are thinking of me? Who thought of
whom first?" It is a very interesting question, and one that
has no simple answer.

When you think of people spontaneously, people you do
not think of often, and out of the clear blue sky you get a
very sharp and clear image of them—then they are

probably thinking of you at the same time. If you have an ongoing relationship with someone and you spend a great deal of time thinking about the person—asking mental questions, talking to or debating with him or her—the person may or may not be thinking of you at the same time. Imagine you are making and sending someone a prerecorded tape as you think of him or her. You do not need to connect at the same instant. The person receives your message when he or she is in a state of receptivity. People may not hear your messages as clearly as they are sent, but they will get them in some way.

Say you are arguing with someone, telling him or her in your mind you do not like the way you are being treated. If the person is highly empathic (able to receive), your message will be heard and you will be aware of an ongoing debate. If the person is not developed telepathically, your thoughts may be received only as a feeling of resentment or anger, and the person may be puzzled or feel angry at what is happening. He or she may not get the transmission the instant you send it, but will play it back like a tape recorded message later when thinking of you and in a receiving state—in a time of silence, reflectiveness, dreaminess, meditation, or any state of quietness of mind. You can compare sending out messages in your mind to dialing a telephone. Nobody can answer you while you are dialing the phone, for the line is tied up. Only after you are finished dialing can you connect with them. When you are thinking of another you are sending out a message. When you are listening you are not sending. You may have noticed that when you are sitting around wanting someone to call, no one calls; but five or six hours later suddenly everyone is calling you. You may be busy and not even thinking of it anymore. It is because usually (although not always) when you send out messages, people take time to receive and act upon them. Just as people do not answer the phone when they are not home, so does it take awhile for people to be silent enough to hear your message. If they are silent, perhaps meditating or daydreaming when you are sending out your message, they may get it instantaneously, and may even act upon it.

When you are deeply connected with and thinking of people, you put your mental communications on a "mental tape" that is available to play when and if they choose. When it comes to receiving messages from others, most of you have not learned that you have the choice of playing them, stopping and starting them, and choosing only those segments you want to hear. Many of you allow whole tapes to play, which can create stress if the recordings are not good ones.

How can you learn to tune into mental tapes and play them when you want? When you think of people, you turn on the tape recorder and allow their communication to come through to you. You have the ability to turn it off at any time by either not thinking of them or by sending them positive loving images, for when you are sending images you cannot receive their thoughts and feelings. If you do not want to hear any recording a friend may have transmitted to you, simply do not think about him. You have the ability to stop thinking of someone by finding things that are interesting and joyful to think of instead. You can send friends high, loving thoughts, pictures of their inner beauty and strength whenever they come into your mind and you will be less affected by their messages.

*It is energizing and fun
to change your thinking habits and
experience new, higher thoughts.*

When you are driving your car, thinking of your errands for the day and your responsibilities, you can also make a conscious effort to think of your higher purpose, your path, and what you can contribute to the world. You can think of those qualities you want to bring into your life—unconditional love, inner peace, wisdom. You may have to consciously choose these thoughts, and train your mind over and over to think of these things rather than your normal thoughts. You may stay at these levels for only a few seconds at first, until your mind gets used to thinking about higher ideals and principles. As you find more enlightened topics to think of, you will shut off your old thinking patterns and the messages that come into you from those levels.

You can use the same technique to turn off the tape recorder. If you do not wish to receive messages from certain people, then do not tune into them. Find things to occupy your mind that energize and bring you joy, and in so doing you will slowly and surely disconnect from their communications.

How can you listen only to the part of the message you want to hear? Take, for example, a case in which you find you get depressed thinking of someone. You get a heavy feeling, or perhaps feel drained when thoughts of her come into your mind. You may feel sorry for her, and wish that she would get her life together. You may be going through a difficult time in your relationship, and find it depresses you to think about her.

To hear only the good part of her recording, make a conscious effort to be centered when you think about her. If you drift into thinking of someone, you open to any messages that come through. However, if you orient yourself before you think of her, focusing on your own energy, feeling relaxed, calm, and confident, you can bring in the more loving message her soul is sending you. If you send your calmness, rather than receiving others' problems, you can control what portion of their communication comes to you. In the case of a person who is draining you, you can choose consciously to send thoughts such as, "I see you as a loving and high being. I want to speak from my soul-self to yours, and I will now open myself to listening to you." If you do not like the feeling of what comes back, you can either shut off your reception of it, or send healing to her.

To send healing, experience your love and compassion for other people. Imagine them getting their lives together in whatever way is appropriate. See their greatness and soul-beauty. Sending healing and loving thoughts will also improve the quality of your telepathic messages. If every time you think of someone you also send a loving, supportive thought, you will find a tremendous difference in the messages that come back to you.

There are ways to stop thinking of a person, if you find you want to.

Consciously focus on things that are fun and joyful to think about. Take the time to develop some joyful images or fantasies, and have them ready whenever the other person pops into your mind. You must intend to stop thoughts of him or her or they will keep coming back. It is a wonderful opportunity to train your mind.

You connect telepathically the most with those you have opened your heart to. It is a challenge to turn off your thoughts when a bond exists at the heart level. If you do not wish to go around hearing the tape recordings that have been sent to you, be aware that every time you allow yourself to think of someone, you are letting yourself receive whatever has been sent out to you. You are also open to receiving whatever feelings the other person is experiencing. If you send a thought of love, you will not bring the other person's energy into yourself.

If you want something from someone and you push the person telepathically to give it to you, you will push him or her away. And the more the person pulls away from you, the more likely you are to push even harder to get through. If someone demands something from you that you don't want to give, you feel "pushed" and your natural reaction is to "pull" away. If you create space within yourself by pulling back and concentrating on your own life and purpose, you will probably find the other person desiring to connect with you. If you want something from people, if you want them to think of you, be with you, or give you attention, the way to get it is by withdrawing all of your attention from them. Most of you do the opposite—you think of someone constantly; you put all your energy into them and the results are exactly the opposite of what you want. They are bombarded with your messages and your energy which is always around them. Why should they seek out your company when you are always with them, on a tape recording, every time their mind relaxes?

If you want attention from someone, make an effort to stop thinking of him or her and get on with your own life. Focus on something else every time you begin to think of the person or send light and see the person dissolving in your mind. Don't check in constantly to see if it is working (is he or she paying attention now?); that is sending the person energy. You must come to the point where you are so involved with your life and work that there is truly a vacuum. When he or she senses you, there is nothing there. Then the person will be drawn to you.

Many of you think that when you want something, and picture somebody giving it to you, you will get it. It usually works in just the opposite way; you create resistance.

If you want something from somebody, picture a time in which you gave that same thing to someone else.

For instance, if you have company staying with you and you want them to help with the housework, remember a time you offered to do housework for people you were staying with. If you want someone to be kinder to you, picture times when you were kind to someone else.

There is a big difference between picturing someone doing something for you and picturing a time when you did that same thing for someone else. Imagine wanting something from somebody, and asking for it over and over, either verbally or in your mind. Most people respond by drawing away. If instead you fill your mind with thoughts of the times you offered those same things, every time he thinks of you he will pick up the pictures you are surrounding yourself with. As he tunes into your pictures, he will begin to think of doing the things you are remembering doing for other people.

How do you handle people who are draining you? First of all, be aware that they could not drain you if you did not give them permission, in some way, to do so. You may say, "I do not want them to drain me," but you are at some level allowing them to do so. If you do not set your own limits and boundaries, they will not set any either. You must say very clearly, "I will not be drained by these people. I will not accept responsibility for their lives," and then you will not be drained. If you do not take responsibility for their well-being they can no longer take your energy. You can, however, send them thoughts of love and peace, which will help them.

Being drained is not caused by telepathic connections as much as by your own beliefs and personality, the decisions you have made about what rights you have and don't have with the people in your life. You can tune out people who make demands of you. If, instead, you feel you owe it to them to hear their complaints, to be there for them even though you don't want to, you will continue to feel drained by them. You may be saying, "There's no way I can disconnect from them." And yet there is, by first affirming to yourself that you *absolutely* have the right to live your own life.

The degree to which you feel responsible for other people's happiness is the degree to which they can pull on you and take from you. They can only use guilt and manipulation because you allow them to by believing you owe them something. If you turn over the responsibility for their lives to them, you won't feel so uncomfortable. You can say to yourself "only they can make themselves powerful, can create good feelings, give to themselves," and then you will no longer feel exhausted by communication with them. They can only pull on you when you feel that they can, when you allow them to take from you because you feel you don't deserve to be left alone.

One person asked me about a neighbor who acted angry and cold, and wasn't responding to the love and good thoughts she was sending him. She wondered what to do with his negative energy. If you are sending people love over and over and they seem to be responding with negative energy or none at all, they may not wish to have you send them energy and love. In this case, the woman needed to withdraw her energy from her neighbor. When she did so, he felt free to seek her out. He was so filled with her energy that he resisted it; it was far more love than he could handle. In fact, she stopped sending him any thoughts and within a month he came over to ask if there was anything he could help her with.

What if you experience a lot of pain when you think of someone, you get an emotional knot that is overwhelming and seems to block out your ability to think loving thoughts? At times, the only way to calm emotions is to turn up the volume of your mind. You can learn to say high words to yourself whether you believe in them or not. You are not drowning out the voice of pain, but turning up the volume of the higher self. Don't make the part of you that is in pain wrong or bad, for that increases its power over you. If it is saying, "This is not working, everything is going wrong, this person has deserted me, or hates me," say high and positive things over and over in your mind. Even if you cannot focus on the words and find your mind going in and out of higher thoughts, persist. The mind can absolutely rule the emotions.

You can calm your emotions by saying inspiring, loving words over and over.

You have been given the gift of thought to help you gain mastery over your lower self. Thought is a useful tool for personal transformation. Your mind is a marvelous instrument, capable of bringing the light of wisdom where there is ignorance and darkness. If you feel overwhelmed by your emotions, begin writing affirmations such as, "The universe is working in perfect harmony. Everything happens for my higher good. I now see a universe of beauty and perfection."

Think these things; say them over and over. Flood your mind with a voice that says, "Things are positive, things are working in my favor, all is order and harmony." The more you fill your mind with positive thoughts, the more you will turn down the volume of your emotions. Affirm spiritual truths and the principles of the soul, such as harmony, balance, and peace. If you keep saying high words, the very vibration of them will begin to calm your emotions. It requires discipline and practice. There are no easy solutions. You must truly intend and will yourself into higher places, then the results you want will follow.

PLAYSHEET

1 | Focus on how you felt when you woke up this morning. How did you feel? What things were on your mind about the day?

2 | Whom did you see or talk to today" How did your energy change before, during and after you saw them? Can you find instances in which you brought in their energy? Make a list of whom you saw and how you felt.

Person I saw: How I felt:

3 | Take any feelings or thoughts you did rot like when you were with him or her and imagine yourself dissolving those emotions and thoughts in light. Breathe deeply and feel yourself returning to a balanced, centered feeling.

XVI

Receiving Guidance
From the Higher Realms

You can learn to receive information from the higher realms of the universe. Just as there are telepathic broadcasts from people, there are many higher broadcasts you can tune into. High levels of guidance and information are available at any time. Just as you cannot see or touch a radio wave, you cannot see or touch these broadcasts—unless you have the will and intent to do so.

What are these broadcasts? There are different levels of information; some involve science, some involve business, teachings of all kinds, visions of peace. All knowledge known and yet to be known is available to you by attuning yourself to these levels. They have been called the universal mind, the collective whole of life-force energy that exists outside of time and space. Many great scientists have tapped this level for their scientific inventions. Many new discoveries, ideas and concepts come from attunement with this frequency. You can bring in information to help you with your business, increase your creativity, or help you become prosperous. Those of you who think of peace on the planet and strive to bring peace into your lives can tap into the broadcast of peace that is available.

A broadcast of healing is available at all times. Its essence is love, compassion, and peace. When you need help, guidance or love it is always available as a broadcast you can tune into to raise your energy and heal whatever needs love. Healers and those in counseling professions often draw from this level in the course of their work; everyone can tune into it. As you attune yourself to this frequency, you feel as if you know what to do or say with a certainty that comes from a level beyond your conscious knowledge.

True healing involves
compassion and love
for both yourself and others.

If you use your hands in bodywork or touch, if you bring through healing information or energy, helping people through your voice, thoughts, or words, you are drawing from this broadcast. Any of you who help others in any way, through your job, family life, or friends, tune into this broadcast of healing and love. Whenever you serve others you pick up this broadcast, and you begin to radiate its healing qualities. As you tune in to these levels of healing you increase your self-love as surely as you increase your ability to heal.

Guidance is also available from many high masters and spirit teachers, both those physically present on the earth and those who are in other realms. Many high souls who are no longer living are holding a focus of peace and love, and are available for personal guidance. You call them guides, for they are there to help hold a high vision for mankind and any person who calls upon them. All of you have a guide, whether you are aware of your guide or not. There are many different ways in which your guide can send you information. Any answers you seek, any information you want, is always there. Information is always being sent to you. Guides wish to help you become aware of your ability to reach higher planes of knowledge and experience, to help you discover your own wisdom and your soul's constant guidance. They will never take away your lessons, but they will help you see what you are learning so that you may move through your growth lessons more quickly. When asked, they can show you an expanded view of any situation, presenting a perspective that allows you to understand what is happening and to act in more loving and compassionate ways. When you view any situation through this wise, expanded perspective it is possible to let go of pain and embrace yourself as a warm and loving person.

*All you need to do
to receive guidance is to
ask for it and then listen.*

You can tune into any of these levels of guidance and information if you have the will and intent to do so. What is will and intent? You may have a picture of your will as that part that says "I will force myself to do this or that." Right use of will is when you love doing something so much that you do it without having to will it or push yourself. You have seen the results when you love to do something, and you have seen what happens when you really don't want to do something but force yourself to do it anyway. You do not produce good results when you make yourself do something or when you have a lot of indecision about it.

Will is a clear focus that is directed towards something you love. The more the focus is undiluted by fears, doubts, and resistance, and is directed like a laser beam to where you want it to go, the greater the ability of the will to draw something to you.

Some of you say you want certain things, think of them often, and then wonder why you do not get them. The more you are uncertain about getting what you want, the longer it takes to get it. When you are clear and your will is focused you bring what you want to you. Imagine that the will, when it wants something, goes out into the universe and finds it, then magnetizes your body towards having it. Will can bring you anything you want, including telepathic reception and connection to the higher realms of the universe.

Those of you who are healers, teachers, or counselors, have a great deal of motivation, intent and desire that makes your healing possible. Healing may be something you consciously chose or something you seemed to "fall into," but to become skilled and good you have had to focus a great deal of your intent and will on it. Will is the dial that tunes you into the right station. There is no magical formula for being a psychic channel, a healer with your hands, mind or words. If you aspire to be anything—a writer, actress, athlete, channel, successful business person—you need only have the will and intent, carried out with action, to do so. The broadcast from the higher levels to guide you to your highest path is always available to any who want and ask for it. Your will to be something or to do something begins to automatically tune you into the broadcast that is appropriate for you.

Many of you would like to be more directly involved in helping people. Many of you are in jobs that you do not feel are aligned with your life purpose. You may wonder if you should be doing something else, if there is some mission you should be fulfilling even though you do not know what it is. The fact that you are thinking these things is an indication that you are a healer and that you do indeed have healing you came here to do. There is no such thing as coincidence or luck in this matter. If you want to find what you are here to do, or if you want to begin your path of serving and healing, the first thing you need to do is decide you are going to do it. The place to start is where you are—serving and helping everyone around you.

If you want to connect with your spirit guide, for instance, all you need to do is decide you will, and ask the universe to lead you to that experience. It will come to you if that is where you put your will, intent, and determination. The degree to which you are sure you want to attract a guide will determine the speed with which you attract one into your life. You may be led to certain books, people, and so forth, to help show you the way.

How do you focus your will? One of the first ways is to remember a time in which you went after a goal and got it. As you think of that past experience, you bring that energy into your present reality. Remember a time in which you were very intent on getting something and you got it. Say you wanted a new car. You went out and looked, you touched cars, drove them, thought about them, read about them and got the money to get one. Look at the level of dedication you put into getting something, and you will see what is required to get something you want now.

Some of the things you wanted may have taken a long time to acquire. You can go back and realize you didn't put a high level of concentration into getting them, or maybe you thought about them infrequently. You may have thought of them often but didn't believe you could have them.

The mind has 40,000 to 50,000 thoughts a day. When 1,000 to 2,000 of those daily thoughts are directed to a goal, it will come rapidly.

Most of you think about something once, maybe two or three times a day, and then you wonder why it takes so long to get it Thoughts are energy. The more you think about something, the more energy you pull from your inner world to create what you think about in the outer world.

The number of thoughts you put into something and the belief or intensity of emotional energy you have about something determines how quickly you create it. The emotional belief you have in getting something is very important. The emotions propel thoughts into reality by the intensity of your belief. The less doubt you have about getting something the more rapidly it will come. Think of a box which represents what you want. Every time you think about what you want the box becomes fuller, and when critical mass is reached the box becomes reality. If there is something you think of over and over, at a certain point it will manifest; how long it takes is based on how much you believe it will come. This does not apply if what you want must come from another person, for you only have control over your reality, not theirs. Wanting something from people which they do not want to give will usually push them away.

The more you can believe you will have something, get excited, picture it in your mind, use your emotions of joy, excitement, and anticipation, the more quickly it will come. But remember that emotions of fear and doubt also create what they focus on, because you are thinking of them over and over. When you fear something, you are thinking of what you do not want to happen, and it fills up a box labeled "What I do not want to happen," and sure enough, that box becomes full and then becomes reality.

If you want to focus your will more clearly, look at your doubts, the things in you that are saying "I cannot have this." There are two boxes here—the box labeled "I can," which is filled with positive thoughts and joyful emotions, and the box labeled "I cannot," which is filled with fears and negative thoughts. If you have many positive thoughts, but they are balanced by equally negative ones, you will create nothing. The desire for what you want must be stronger than your fears about having it. Every time you fear something, you take away from the energy you are putting out to create it. Don't make those fear thoughts wrong, but every time you recognize one, put positive thoughts alongside it.

After you are clear that you want to receive guidance, and you intend to do so, feeling positive and excited about it, you will then receive it. Reception of the broadcast takes place outside the mind and happens in a flash. By the time your mind becomes aware of an idea, the information has already come into your higher centers; you have already received it.

If you look upward and focus on higher realms, as surely as you breathe you will receive any help or information you need.

The experience of the higher realms often comes in the form of *inner seeing*. All of you have had the experience of inner knowing, a sixth sense, a feeling that something was going to happen—and it did. You might have an awareness, for instance, that a person you are with isn't well. Sometimes you look at people and you know something about them that you couldn't possibly know except by some added dimension of insight.

You have constant insights and revelations and new thoughts about your life. Telepathic messages are received instantaneously, and there is no conscious awareness of their reception. I cannot tell you how to be aware of your telepathic reception of higher guidance, for it occurs outside of awareness. You first become aware of it through your thoughts and your inner seeing. Suddenly you have a new way of handling a problem, or a change in your consciousness, which is the first indication most of you have that you have received the broadcast. As this guidance comes into your emotional self you soon find that old situations no longer trigger the emotional response they used to. As you bring the broadcast into your heart you find yourself expanding and able to feel love and forgiveness where you didn't before. You begin communicating ideas to others in new and different ways. As you bring it into your body, you often change your physical body or your awareness of it.

The information is always there; the only block is your lack of will and intent to receive the broadcast. If you wish to receive more knowledge, all you need to do is make the *decision* to do so and focus upon it. When you find yourself thinking mundane thoughts that go nowhere, taking time that you could spend in higher ways, think instead about the issue you want more information about. Then get silent for a few moments and open to receive the broadcast. You will find some new bit of information or insight within an hour or two. It is easy to receive from the universal mind; all you need to do is want to receive. The information may come to you through a friend or book; you may hear it or see it. It may come in the form of a new thought. You can direct it better by becoming silent, going into a relaxed state, and quieting your mind. It is important to acknowledge that it *has* come. By connecting it with your will and intent you strengthen your belief in your ability to create.

You are independent individuals who determine your own lives and destiny by your will and intent. The more aware you are of the connection between what you want and its arrival, the more you will find your ability to create what you want increasing. Whenever you have a new idea or a new thought, and acknowledge it, you open to receiving more.

Writing down your goals brings them to you faster.

What you want may be knowledge, an increased opportunity to serve, or the desire to be a psychic channel, for instance. It may be a business opportunity, a new career, anything you want. Write down your intent and make it a clear message to the universe, "I intend to write a book" or "I intend to discover my psychic and healing abilities, and I am now doing so." The clearer you can be that you do want to go in a certain direction, the more quickly you can bring it about. You will begin to draw to you much information and guidance.

Another way is to affirm to yourself when you are in a quiet space that you would like new insights about your work. Be willing to recognize new insights, and then let go of the request. Monitor what comes into your thoughts in the next half day or even half hour, just to experience what it feels like to receive from the higher levels.

Many have asked me, "How can I know the difference between my thoughts and the higher thoughts of the universe?" For you wonder, "Was that a revelation, an inspiration, or was that my own mind thinking a wise thought?" There is no difference. The telepathic reception of higher levels of knowledge is beyond your level of conscious awareness. You first become aware of it when it hits your thought processes. Some of you are aware of it sooner, such as when you are healing someone and you sense energy. There are other ways of becoming aware of it, but the actual reception is beyond the scope of knowing. So you are asking, "How do I recognize it? How do I receive better?" If you want to receive better, if that is your desire, then you will. If you want to become more aware of your reception of guidance, then you will.

Every time you have a thought that seems to be outside of your normal range—for instance, you may be walking down the street and suddenly you come up with a new idea—you have received information from a higher realm. Many of you expect to hear a voice out of the sky telling you something; it is not usually that kind of experience. It usually feels like your own mind or imagination. By the time you are aware of reception, the information is already in your world of form, which is your thoughts and your body. The ideas feel like your own thoughts, but they have a higher quality to them. They are of a different nature; they bring a new way of looking at something or a more loving perspective. When you have a new thought, that is a sign that you are in tune with that higher level of guidance. The more you validate it, the more you acknowledge that you picked up telepathic messages, the more you will continue to get them. You will find that it becomes more and more boring to think at your old levels; you get tired of running the same problems around in your mind when it can be so rewarding to receive inspiration and insights. Boredom is often a tool of the soul to lure you into new spaces.

If you want to bring in guidance more directly, perhaps connecting with your own guide, start by sitting quietly.

There are many altered states of consciousness you experience in the normal course of the day. When you get lost in a book, when you watch TV, when you drift off to the sounds of beautiful music, when you daydream, paint, or play a musical instrument, you are in a state of altered consciousness. These states are associated with the right brain, your creative nature, and are the states that most contribute to receiving higher guidance. Guidance is received through the right or creative side of the brain; it is then translated through the left-brain side of memory and logic into concrete information. Whenever you get quiet, you are in a more receptive state.

Your challenge at these times is to tune out mundane and idle thoughts and focus your attention upward. When you think of other people in this quiet state of receptivity, you can receive their emotional or mental energy. If they are depressed or in pain you may lower your own energy as you think of them. When you receive telepathically from the higher levels of the universe, you move up into your higher self. As you become more loving and full of light, you can bring up the energy of others also. They may not go as high (or some may go higher) but you can raise the vibration of everyone around you by tuning your awareness higher.

As you sit quietly, ask for guidance. Then, be willing to listen. Notice your body. Perhaps you will feel a physical sensation like a tingling as you focus upward. Ask for guidance, stating clearly your question. Keep random thoughts from pulling on your attention. If you can focus for even five minutes on what you want guidance on, you will receive a new way of thinking, a higher outlook in that short space. Your call is always heard; the only problem comes in your ability to listen.

How do you broadcast healing to others? You touch people you speak to them, you write and send out your knowledge. When it is your intent to connect with others from your higher centers, your words, writings and touch come from that place. You may say, "How do I know if I am saying the right words, touching the body in just the right way for healing?" If the intent is to be healing, then the words and the touch will always be right for that person. There is no error at this level. Only your mind and personality can create judgment and error. Whenever you have the intent to heal, no matter what process you use, what form or technique you try, you will be healing. The other person must also want the healing, for if they are not ready then nothing you try will work.

If, however, you are feeling angry, and want to get back at someone, then your intent is clearly not healing. If you try to speak nice words to cover your anger, you are not healing. There is no lying at this level. If you walk around with the intent to heal, then everywhere you go—the grocery store, the office—you will be a healing influence, even though you may not be doing so consciously.

It *is up to you*
to create the specific form
your work will take.

The guidance that is available to you is unlimited in whatever form you choose and whatever field you choose, be it business, the healing arts, performing arts, science, education, or others. The will to do anything magnetizes you to the information and guidance you need in that area. The main function of the higher centers of telepathy is to attune you with your higher purpose, help you discover what you came to earth to do, and bring to you the information you need to do it. As you experience working in these higher levels, you will increase your ability to be a loving influence on those around you, and increase your ability to see with your inner eyes. The intent to do so is all that is necessary to attune yourself to the higher realms of guidance.

PLAYSHEET

1 | Think of five things—a decision, problem, or choice—that you asked for guidance on last year and received.

2 | Think of something you want guidance on right now in your life. Sit quietly, ask for guidance, and notice if any new thoughts come in. Record them here.

Companion Books
by Orin and DaBen

By Orin

LuminEssence Productions • P.O. Box 1310 • Medford, OR 97501 • USA

BOOK I OF THE SOUL LIFE SERIES
Soul Love: Awakening Your Heart Centers
In *Soul Love*, Orin's first book of the Soul Life Series, you will meet and blend with your soul. You will learn more about your chakras and how to work with your soul and the Beings of Light to awaken your heart centers. When these centers are awakened and working together in a triangle of light, you can more easily experience soul love, peace, joy, bliss, and aliveness. Discover how to attract a soul mate, soul link, make heart connections, create soul relationships, change personality love into soul love, and lift all the energies about you into your heart center to be purified and transformed. See results in your life when you use Orin's easy, step-by-step processes to heal your heart of past hurts, to open to receive more love, and to bring all your relationships to a higher level. (H J Kramer, Inc, 252 pages)

By Orin and DaBen

Opening to Channel: How to Connect With Your Guide
By Sanaya Roman and Duane Packer
Orin and DaBen – a wise and healing spirit teacher channeled by Duane Packer – will teach you how to connect with and verbally channel a high-level guide. Channeling is a skill that can be learned, and Sanaya and Duane have successfully trained thousands to channel using these safe, simple and effective processes. You will learn what channeling is and how to know if you are ready to channel, go into trance, receive information clearly, what to expect in your first meeting with your guide, and much more. (H J Kramer, Inc, 264 pages)

Creating Money: Keys to Abundance
By Sanaya Roman and Duane Packer
Learn how to follow the spiritual laws of money and abundance, use advanced manifesting techniques, and create what you want. You will learn how to discover and draw your life's work to you. This book contains many simple techniques, positive affirmations, and exercises to help you create rapid changes in your prosperity. Abundance is your natural state, and as you use the information in this book you will learn how to let money and abundance flow readily into your life while doing what you love. You can develop unlimited thinking, listen to your inner guidance, and transform your beliefs. Discover how to work with energy to easily create what you want and tap into the unlimited abundance of the universe. (H J Kramer, Inc, 282 pages)

More from Orin

Audio Cassette Tape Albums by Orin

These *Personal Power Through Awareness* guided meditations by Orin in Volumes I and II will help you put into practice the techniques in this book as well as teach you many new skills. They will develop your ability to be aware of energy and to create the future you want. These tapes make an excellent course to study on your own, or use them to conduct your own classes.

Personal Power Through Awareness – Volume I: Sensing Energy by Orin. In this first volume you will learn how to create the reality you want using energy, thought, and tools of light. These guided journeys develop your skills of visualizing, sensing and affecting the energy around you, and increasing your intuitive abilities and your ability to receive higher guidance. Includes: Sensing Energy; Sensing Unseen Energy; Sensing Energy in Others; Who Am I?– Sensing Your Own Energy; Developing Intuition; Evolving Emotional Telepathy; Sending and Receiving Telepathic Images; and Receiving Higher Guidance. Set of four tapes with eight processes in attractive cassette album. *P201 $59.95*** *(Individual tapes not sold separately; free tape offer does not apply to albums.)*

Personal Power Through Awareness – Volume II: Journey Into Light by Orin. The processes in this album contain powerful techniques to transform your experience of yourself and your life. Each journey teaches you how to create the future you want in various areas of your life. You will experience yourself in new, higher ways, learn how to love yourself more, come from your power, stay in your center around others, and more. Includes: Learning Unconditional Love; Handling Pain – Transforming Negative Energy; Bringing Your Unconscious Into Consciousness; Journey Into Light – Going Higher; Self-Love – Evolving Your Inner Dialogue; Transforming Your Inner Images; Finding Your Deepest Truth; and Wisdom – Being Your Higher Self. Set of four tapes with eight processes in attractive cassette album. *P202 $59.95*** *(Individual tapes not sold separately; free tape offer does not apply to albums.)*

**Buy both Volumes I and II (P201 and P202) at the same time for $99.95 and save $19.95. Specify *P203* on order. *(Free tape offer does not apply to albums.)*

Receive a Free Subscription to our Newsletter

To receive a FREE subscription to our newsletter with messages from Orin about current earth changes, information on the energies present and how to work with them, as well as information about tapes and seminars, write to LuminEssence Productions at the address below, visit our website at www.orindaben.com, or send in the card at the back of this book. Be sure to include your name, address, and phone number.

LuminEssence Productions • P.O. Box 1310 • Medford, OR 97501 • USA

Audio Cassette Tapes

A Message from Orin About These Guided Meditation Tapes

"I offer these guided meditations to you who have read my books and want to go further, using and living these principles. Working with guided meditations, where your mind is in a relaxed, open state, is one of the most powerful ways known to create rapid, profound, and lasting changes in your life. Many of you who are drawn to my books are 'old' evolved souls, and I have used processes and techniques that I feel are most effective for people at your soul level. I have carefully selected the processes, words, and images on the tapes to awaken you to who you are. These guided meditations contain powerful and effective tools of light to create positive changes in your life. I transmit energy to you directly through my voice. I work with your Higher Self, conscious mind, and subconscious mind for lasting changes. I offer these meditations to you who want to take a quantum leap, accelerate your growth, and live a life of joy rather than struggle." *– Orin*

Personal Power Through Awareness Affirmations Side 1, Guided Journey Side 2 (P100) Based on the book's principles.
Past-Life Regression (SI043)   **Being Your Higher Self** (SI040)
Discovering Your Life Purpose – What Am I Here to Do? (L104)
Developing Intuition (010)   **Age Regression** (SI041)
Radiating Unconditional Love (P103)
Self-Love (L102)   **Overcoming the Self-Destruct** (SI060)
Opening Your Psychic Abilities (013)   **Opening to Receive** (L106)
Lucid Dreaming (SI024)   **Reprogramming at Cellular** (SI056)
Clearing Blockages (SI057)   **Taking a Quantum Leap** (L103)
Losing Weight, Looking Younger (SI030)
Attracting Your Soul Mate (RE002)   **Meeting Your Spirit Guide** (014)
For Self-Employed: Creating Money, Clients, Sales (SI037)
Having What You Want in a Relationship (RE003)

All tapes include beautiful music by Thaddeus with same journey on both sides except as noted. Tapes listed above are $9.98 each.

Books by Orin
Published by H J Kramer, Inc

Living with Joy: Keys to Personal Power and Spiritual Transformation by Sanaya Roman, channel for Orin. Book I of the Earth Life Series. *LWJ* $12.95

Spiritual Growth: Being Your Higher Self by Sanaya Roman, channel for Orin. Book II of the Earth Life Series. *SG* $12.95

Soul Love: Awakening Your Heart Centers by Sanaya Roman, channel for Orin. Book I of the Soul Life Series by Orin. *SL* $12.95

Opening to Channel: How to Connect with Your Guide by Sanaya Roman and Duane Packer, channels for Orin and DaBen. *OTC* $12.95

Creating Money: Keys to Abundance by Sanaya Roman and Duane Packer, channels for Orin and DaBen. *CM* $12.95

LuminEssence Productions • www.orindaben.com

Additional Resources

Audio Cassette Tape Albums by Orin

Opening to Channel. This audio cassette tape course by Orin and DaBen (channeled by Duane Packer) is to help you open to channel. Processes include: Relaxation, focus, and concentration techniques; Journey to the Higher Realms to prepare you for your opening; Trance posture; Opening to verbal channeling; Questions to ask your guide in trance; Instructions for giving yourself a reading; and Learning how to give readings to others. Set of 4 tapes with more than 16 processes in album. *C100 $49.95*

Creating Money. These audio cassette prosperity tapes by Orin are for creating an abundant reality. Processes include: Magnetizing Yourself (SI010); Clearing Beliefs and Old Programs (SI071); Releasing Doubts and Fears (SI075); Linking with Your Soul and the Guides (SI076); Aura Clearing, Energy and Lightwork (SI073); Awakening Your Prosperity Self (SI074); Success (SI070); and Creating Abundance (SI072). All tapes are $9.98 each. For a set of all 8 processes (4 two-sided tapes in album), order the Creating Money Album and save. *M100 $49.95*

Transformation: Evolving Your Personality, by Orin. These meditations assist you in handling the challenges that come from being on an accelerated path of spiritual growth such as blockages, mood swings, old issues coming up, overstimulation, etc. Meditations include: Self-Appreciation; Honoring Your Path of Awakening; Focusing Inward: Hearing Your Soul's Voice; Focusing Upward: Hearing the Voice of the Masters and Guides; Reparenting Yourself: Changing the Past; Creating the Future with Light; Beyond Intellect: Opening Your Higher Mind; and Journey to the Temple of the Masters to reprogram at cellular, release limitations, old beliefs, blockages, and more. Set of 4 tapes with 8 meditations. *SG200 $49.95 (Tapes not sold separately.)*

Awakening Your Light Body: Keys to Enlightenment
A Six-Volume, Audio Cassette Course by Orin and DaBen

Orin and DaBen's *Awakening Your Light Body* tape course contains extensive written material and six audio-cassette tape albums (containing 72 tape journeys) to take you on a step-by-step spiritual growth program. This is recommended for you who have studied metaphysics and have been on a growth path for awhile, and are ready for your spiritual growth to become an even more important part of your life. If you want to learn how to sense energy at a very refined level; are ready to experience many heightened, expanded states of consciousness; want to open your channel upward; learn how to create with energy; and take a quantum leap, write or call for information on our *Awakening Your Light Body* tape course. The positive life changes and results this course has created for people have been beyond anything we imagined possible.

Write for a Free Subscription to our Newsletter

To receive a FREE subscription to our newsletter with a message from Orin about current earth changes, as well as information about tapes and seminars, write to LuminEssence Productions at the address below. Be sure to include your name, address, and phone number.

LuminEssence Productions • P.O. Box 1310 • Medford, OR 97501 • USA

LuminEssence Productions • P.O. Box 1310 • Medford, OR 97501

To order by phone with Visa/Mastercard call (541) 770-6700,
fax (541) 770-6632, or visit our website at www.orindaben.com

Order Form

BUY THREE $9.98 TAPES AND GET A FOURTH $9.98 TAPE FREE!!
(Free tape offer does not apply to tape albums.)

Your Name _____
(Please print)

Address _____

City_____ State _____ Zip _____

Country _____

Daytime   Email
Telephone: (_____)_____ Address: _____
(Telephone required for international shipments.) (In case we have questions about your order.)

QTY	ITEM	DESCRIPTION	PRICE

Shipping and Handling Fees:
(Rates are subject to change.)

Subtotal:	U.S.A.		International Air Mail		
	U.P.S.	First Class U.S. Mail	Canada	Other International	
Up to $10	$5.95	$3.05	$3.85	$6.80	
$11 to $50	$6.45	$6.50	$6.65	$11.70	
$51 to $89	$7.10	$7.15	$7.85	$18.30	
$90 to $100	$7.75	$7.85	$8.90	$23.15	
$101 to $200	$8.30	$9.10	$10.95	$29.10	
Over $200	$11.40	$13.05	$21.20	$45.60	

Subtotal _____
Shipping _____
TOTAL _____

Thank You
for
Your Order!

☐ U.S.A. orders shipped UPS unless box is checked.
(UPS cannot deliver to PO Box addresses.)

Payment enclosed: ☐ Check   ☐ Money Order

Please charge my: ☐ Visa   ☐ Mastercard

Credit Card No. _____ Exp. Date_____

Signature as on card _____

Please make check payable to **LuminEssence Productions**. Remember to allow time for U.S. Mail or UPS delivery after order is shipped. All orders shipped within two business days of receipt. Incomplete orders will be returned. **International orders** payable in U.S. Funds drawn ON a U.S. bank. All international orders will be shipped by air mail. For international orders, we prefer payment by credit card if possible.   P16

Come Visit our Website at
www.orindaben.com

"Many of you are beginning to tune your consciousness to the oneness of the higher dimensions where all life is connected. One of the outer manifestations of this is the worldwide web. If you are not already connected to it, we encourage you to do so. It is rapidly expanding the consciousness and potential of humanity, and is an important evolutionary step." —Orin and DaBen

Come visit and enjoy connecting with us as you visit our website. You can read and have fun in various ways:

- Read more about Orin and Sanaya Roman.
- Receive a personal daily affirmation; pick from a number of topics and receive a personal affirmation for that area.
- Read and send to others Orin's newsletter articles on such topics as the energies present now until 2012, Orin comments on prophecies, articles on creating abundance, and more.
- Read excerpts from other Orin books.
- Read about channeling, how to recognize a high-level guide, more about what is conscious channeling, and take a quiz to determine if you might be ready to channel.
- Learn about joining Sanaya and Orin on the inner planes on Sunday mornings for meditations and a worldwide call to the great ones to ask for their assistance in uplifting humanity.
- Take a "light break" during the day and listen to various short meditations by Orin on topics such as self-love, clearing blockages, clear and creative thinking, receiving abundance, relaxation, feeling energized, loving relationships, radiating unconditional love, cellular activation, and more.
- Read a wonderful weekly meditation and book excerpt.
- Read about Orin and DaBen's *Awakening Your Light Body* course and take a short quiz to determine if you might be ready to awaken your light body.
- Read information about teaching the *Personal Power Through Awareness* book as classes.
- Read Orin's current newsletter on-line.
- Sign the guestbook and give your feedback.

Join Us for Our Worldwide Meditations

Participate in our global linkups on the inner planes. Join us to call upon the Great Ones to request their assistance for ourselves and for humanity. You can also join us on the inner planes during our regular Sunday-morning meditations from 9:15–9:30 a.m., California (USA) time. Use whatever meditation practice you are familiar with, and add your light to the group light we all create together. For more information, send for our free newsletter at the address below, or visit our website at www.orindaben.com.

LuminEssence Productions • P.O. Box 1310 • Medford, OR 97501 • USA